The burning of Knockcroghery village, Co. Roscommon, 1921

Maynooth Studies in Local History

SERIES EDITOR Michael Potterton

This is one of six volumes in the Maynooth Studies in Local History series for 2022. It is also my first year as series editor, having taken over the role from the irreplaceable Raymond Gillespie, who held that position from 1995 to 2021, overseeing the publication of a veritable treasure trove of studies in those 27 years. Raymond established the series with Irish Academic Press as a direct result of the enormous success of the Maynooth MA in Local History programme, which began in 1992. Under Raymond's supervision, some 153 volumes were produced, authored by 140 different scholars (94 men and 46 women). The first volume, on education in nineteenth-century Meath, was written by Paul Connell, and the 153rd, on the Dublin Cattle Market in the 1950s and 1960s, was by Declan O'Brien. Eleven people have each contributed two volumes to the series, while Terry Dooley is the only person to have written three.

The remarkable collection now covers some 1,500 years of history across 31 counties, dealing variously with aspects of agriculture and fishing, architecture, crime and punishment, death and burial, economy and trade, education, famine, gender, healthcare, industry, language and literature, migration, music and the arts, politics, religion, society, travel and communication, urban development, war and much more besides. I am grateful to Raymond for entrusting the series to me, and to Four Courts Press for not vetoing the appointment. Together, I am sure that we can build on the sound foundations established over more than quarter of a century of diligent work.

The current crop of titles takes us from a broad look at religion and society in medieval Galway to a very specific and tragic event in Knockcroghery village on the night of 20 June 1921. En route we witness the gradual dismantling of Irish lordship in early modern north Co. Cork, and the development of nursing and midwifery in Co. Tipperary at the turn of the twentieth century. Finally, we have biographical sketches of two remarkable men of the nineteenth century – Thomas Conolly (1823–76) of Castletown House in Co. Kildare and botanist Nathaniel Colgan (1851–1919) of Dublin.

While the genesis and home of this series lie firmly at Maynooth, it is a mark of its appeal, its breadth and its inclusivity that this year's contributors are drawn from Carlow College, Glenstal Abbey, NUI Galway, Trinity College Dublin and the University of Limerick as well as Maynooth University.

Maynooth Studies in Local History: Number 155

The burning of Knockcroghery village, Co. Roscommon, 1921

Regina Donlon

FOUR COURTS PRESS

Set in 11.5pt on 13.5pt Bembo by
Carrigboy Typesetting Services for
FOUR COURTS PRESS LTD
7 Malpas Street, Dublin 8, Ireland
www.fourcourtspress.ie
and in North America for
FOUR COURTS PRESS
c/o IPG, 814 N Franklin Street, Chicago, IL 60610

ISBN 978–1–80151–030–1

Printed in Ireland
by SprintPrint, Dublin

Contents

Acknowledgments

On a dark autumn afternoon in 2002, my then history teacher, the inimitable Mary Higgins, mooted the idea of identifying a special research topic for our Leaving Certificate exam. With this, my interest in the burning of Knockcroghery began and so it seems fitting that twenty years later, my first words of thanks are to her.

There are a number of people that helped this project come to fruition. I am indebted to Dr Michael Potterton, the series editor of the Maynooth Studies in Local History series, for giving me the opportunity to tell this story, and for his understanding and flexibility throughout the process.

Attempting to finalize a piece of research during a pandemic presents a unique set of challenges, but the efficiency and professionalism of Ian Strawbridge at the National Archives, Kew, Selina Collard at the UCD archives, Dublin and the staff at Roscommon County Library made the process significantly easier and for that I am very grateful.

There are several local historians that have trodden this path before me and their work and knowledge has been invaluable in piecing this story together. Their foresight in interviewing people in the community who lived through the burning has preserved a unique element of our collective past and I owe them a great debt of gratitude. They are Riona Egan, Declan Coyne and William Gacquin. A very special word of thanks to Mary Murray Dwyer whose passion for local history is as infectious as her knowledge of it. Mary was instrumental in guiding me through the early part of this research and in helping to piece together the events of that night.

I would also like to thank Dr Elaine Callinan and Dr Noel Kavanagh at Carlow College, St Patrick's, for their support, knowledge and encouragement as this project unfolded. Similarly, Olive Kilcommons and Martha and Glenn Naughton lived through this project with me and at times were required to be confidants, strategists and taskmasters, roles at which they each excelled.

Finally and most especially, there are three people who have made considerable sacrifices so that I could complete this work. To my husband, Stephen and our daughter, Emily, thank you for taking care of each other while I disappeared for hours upstairs and thank you for being there with a smile when I returned.

My biggest debt of gratitude is to my mother, Elizabeth, who introduced me to this story, and who was and is my first, biggest and most enduring supporter. Thank you. This book is dedicated to her.

Introduction

On a bright Monday evening in late June 1921, Colonel-Commandant Thomas Stanton Lambert and his wife, Geraldine, together with their travelling companions, Colonel Challoner, his wife and his niece, were returning from a lawn tennis party at Killinure House (fig. 1). The house, owned by Peter Ponsonby Metge, was situated on the eastern shores of Lough Ree, approximately 15km north of Victoria Barracks in Athlone, Co. Westmeath, the party's intended destination.[1] However, approaching 7.30p.m. at Benown, near Glasson, their motor car was ambushed and Lambert, the commanding officer of the 13th Infantry Brigade was assassinated. The ambush, an attempted kidnapping gone awry, had profound consequences for the unsuspecting population of a small village to the north of Athlone on the western shore of Lough Ree. Within hours of Lambert's death, the village of Knockcroghery was ablaze, the local population was homeless and the economy destroyed. Ironically, the burning of Knockcroghery, an act of retribution in Lambert's name, was ultimately a case of mistaken identity.

The village of Knockcroghery, Co. Roscommon, is situated on the main thoroughfare between the former market towns of Athlone and Roscommon. It is bordered on the east by the shores of Lough Ree and is situated in the civil parish of Killinvoy. Today, the village is the largest settlement in the Catholic parish of Knockcroghery, St John's and Rahara. The origins of the village are said to pre-date the mid-seventeenth century when the settlement was known as *An Creagán*, or 'Stoney hill', a reference to the hill north of the village. By the time the Down Survey was completed in the mid-1650s, however, the village was widely known as Knockcroghery, or *Cnoc na Chrocaire*, 'the hill of the hanging'.[2] The hanging in question was that of the O'Ceallaigh clan of nearby Galey Castle, who had resisted Sir Charles Coote's attack on the castle during the Cromwellian conquest in 1651.[3] Throughout the eighteenth century, the settlement continued to develop and over time became known as an area that excelled in

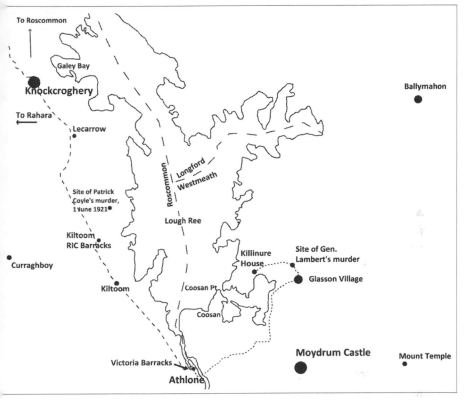

1. Map identifying areas of interest during the War of Independence in the south Roscommon/Westmeath area, June 1921
(base-map source: OSI National Townland and Historical Map Viewer available at: https://geohive.maps.arcgis.com/, last accessed 18 Apr. 2022)

clay-pipe production. By the nineteenth century, this industry, along with agriculture, were the two main pillars on which the local economy stood. The paucity of nineteenth-century source material frustrates any attempt to reconstruct the economic profile of the village to any great extent, but the production of clay pipes was integral to the continued development and prosperity of the area. As the twentieth century dawned, and new ways of consuming tobacco were becoming more popular, clay-pipe production in the area still retained a significant market share as the pipes were relatively cheap to produce and, as a result, were also relatively cheap to purchase. By 1900, the clay pipe had become known as the pipe of the common man and they were popular accessories at fairs, markets, wakes, weddings and many other social events. However, production of the Knockcroghery clay pipe came to an abrupt end on the night of 20–1 June 1921 as the village was targeted by crown forces in a reprisal attack for the murder of Colonel-Commandant Lambert earlier that evening.

This study proposes to examine the events of that night and the days that followed, and explores how and why Knockcroghery was targeted. In so doing, the experiences of the residents of the village are also considered against the backdrop of complex military and political antagonisms at both local and national levels. This, in turn, necessitates an investigation of the War of Independence in the area, or perhaps more specifically in the region, to ascertain how a murder on the eastern shore of Lough Ree was avenged on the western shore.

The concept of regionality in this investigation is an important one. Charles Townshend, Joost Augusteijn and David FitzPatrick have explored this phenomenon and their perspectives are well established in the discourse.[4] More recently, Marie Coleman and John Burke, among a plethora of others, have offered examinations of regionality during the Irish revolutionary period. In the studies mentioned above, the interconnectedness of Longford, Westmeath and Roscommon during this period is well articulated.[5] Indeed, it is important to overlook the county boundaries in this current investigation as events in Longford and Westmeath directly impacted the reprisal that was levied on Knockcroghery in June 1921 by crown forces.

There is no doubt that the burning of the village was a watershed moment in the War of Independence in the region and a communal trauma grew out of the events of that night. Jimmy Murray recalls that when people in the community were referring to particular events, the phrase 'before the burning' or 'after the burning' was used. However, for the most part, descendants of the families involved regularly state that 'it just wasn't talked about'. Indeed, even in the days and weeks after the burning took place it seems that it just wasn't talked about. The local newspapers, those published in Athlone and in Roscommon, imposed a type of self-censorship in the weeks and months after the burning. This, presumably, was an act of self-preservation borne out of a fear of reprisal should they condemn the sacking. Therefore the story of the burning of Knockcroghery was told mainly through the national press where it was opportunistically politicized and integrated into broader political narratives.

Moreover, other sources specific to the period, for example the Bureau of Military History witness statements, are also lacking significant accounts of the burning. Although members of the 4th South Roscommon Brigade were interviewed and even though the burning is mentioned, very little detail is actually provided. The official record of the time is, perhaps predictably, scant as evidenced by the three-line report sent to Dublin Castle the day after the burning and the reports of the county inspector that followed.[6] Very little written material exists at local level that documents the burning and even the diaries of local farmer Benjamin Greene are available for 1920 and 1922–4 and beyond, but the diary for 1921 is missing.[7] Similarly, the *Roscommon Messenger*, the predominant newspaper in the area, is also missing for 1921, and so even now, the burning of the village is difficult to talk about.

Despite the frustrating lack of source material, there are a number of dedicated local historians and descendants of the families that have unique experiences to share. One of the most important sources for this work are interviews given in the early 2000s by local man, Jimmy Murray, who was 4 years old at the time of the sacking. Murray's was one of only three homes to survive on the night of the attack. In 2003, Murray did an extended interview with Declan Coyne which was published in the *75th Anniversary Magazine of the Roscommon Champion* and this has proven to be an invaluable source in piecing together the events of the night.[8] Local historian William Gacquin has written extensively on the history of south Roscommon and the burning of Knockcroghery features in some of his research, while more recently, to commemorate the centenary of the burning of the village in 2021, locals have produced a documentary entitled *The burning of Knockcroghery, 1921*, which includes numerous interviews with descendants.[9]

In local lore and in some of the printed source material, both primary and secondary, the Black and Tans are named as the perpetrators of the attack. The use of this terminology in the context of Knockcroghery is problematic for a number of reasons. First, as the assailants arrived in the village in civilian clothing and as nobody was ever held accountable for the attack, it is impossible to deduce that it was in fact members of the Black and Tans that did initiate the burning of the village. Second, the phrase 'Black and Tans' is inflammatory, even today, and so unless used in the correct context, the phrase engenders a specific emotional response and evokes confrontational imagery. Therefore, a conscious decision has been taken in this research to avoid the use of the term, simply because it cannot be proven that it was the Black and Tans that burned the village, even though history, as well as the contemporary press, have assumed it was. The exception, of course, is when this phrase is used as part of quoted source material. Perhaps the issue lies in the generic use of the term 'Black and Tans', employed, as it often is, as an umbrella term when what are actually being referred to are the British authorities more generally. In this study, the term 'crown forces' is utilized unless a specific agent is identifiable.

The following chapters tell the story of the burning of Knockcroghery and explore the complex world of rural Ireland through the lens of the final weeks of the War of Independence in the region. In so doing, it demonstrates how local communities were impacted by evolving national narratives, while also engaging with economic, social and political antagonisms characteristic of the era.

1. The village

As Isaac Weld entered the village of Knockcroghery in the early 1830s, he noted that

> The approach to the village is rather pleasing and the street up the hill is spacious and airy ... The village is prosperous owing to its little manufactory of tobacco pipes, which gives employment and brings in a moderate income to several families.[1]

He went on to note that the village consisted of approximately forty-five dwelling houses, of which three were slated. These dwellings catered to a population of approximately 180.[2] A mill in a poor state of repair was situated on the stream to the north of the village, but this eyesore was counter-balanced by the presence of a new Roman Catholic church and schoolhouse, 'which contribute[d] very materially to the improved appearance of the place'.[3]

There was evidence of a glebe house and church as well as a RIC station.[4] The fair green was situated to the north of the village and large fairs were held three times during the year, on 26 May, 21 August and 25 October.[5] The October fair was recorded by Samuel Lewis as being 'a large sheep fair', while George S. Measom compared the 'great' October fair in Knockcroghery with the more widely known October fair in Ballinasloe.[6] In the decades after Weld's visit, a train station was established, which handled both freight and passengers from its foundation in February 1863 until its closure in June 1963, and the village was a stop on the main Dublin–Westport railway line, which was operated by the Midland Great Western Railway.[7]

In his synopsis, Weld captured the essence of the village eloquently and it remained largely in this state until the turn of the twentieth century. By 1901, the population of Knockcroghery was relatively young and records exist for eighty-seven people resident in the village itself. Of these, over three-quarters were under the age of fifty.[8] A decade later, seventy-seven people were enumerated in an area defined as 'Knockcroghery town' by census enumerators, and 90 per cent of the village's population were less than fifty years of age. Moreover, the census abstracts for 1926 indicate that Scregg DED, in which Knockcroghery was located, actually recorded a 5 per cent increase in its population between 1911 and 1926.[9] This is a surprising trend given the rise in the levels of emigration from rural Ireland in the early decades of the century, coupled with the fate that befell the village on a warm summer's night in June 1921.[10]

The denominational composition of the area was relatively diverse and included Roman Catholics, Church of Ireland worshippers and Baptists. Unsurprisingly, the community was predominately Catholic, and in the early decades of the century the position of parish priest was held by two brothers from Mantua near Elphin.[11] Having originally served as curate in the half parish St John's, Fr Michael Kelly was the parish priest of the Knockcroghery, St John's and Rahara from 1907 to 1919. However, after his untimely death, he was succeeded by his brother, Fr Bartley Kelly. Fr Bartley had a very cordial relationship with his Church of Ireland counterpart, Revd Mr Thomas S. Humphries, who himself was relatively new to the village having succeeded Revd Mr Thomas Irwin in the position of rector. For the most part, a tolerant community dynamic was visible. There were a number of Protestant families in the area including, among others, the Jacksons in Knockcroghery village, the Munroes of Gailey House and the Greenes, who were resident at Hill House, Lecarrow. In his diary for the year 1920, Benjamin Greene recorded receiving a cheque from Fr Kelly 'for £2 8s. for potatoes and service of cows', highlighting the interdependence and cooperation between both denominational groups.[12] Greene offered another example of this just over a month later when he recorded that he had 'dipped 100 sheep at Denis O'Brien's, Knockcroghery at 2d. per sheep and paid 16/8'.[13]

THE LOCAL ECONOMY

Both Lewis and Weld noted that the main industry in the area was the manufacture of clay pipes for tobacco and there is little doubt that this activity sustained a significant portion of the village's population.[14] Reliance on this industry, therefore, compounded the level of destruction experienced by the people of Knockcroghery on the morning of 21 June 1921 when word of the village's fate began to emerge. During his visit to the village in the 1830s, Weld became interested in the process of clay-pipe production, noting that

> it is somewhat remarkable that the village in itself affords nothing peculiarly favourable to the manufacture [of clay pipes], the clay not being found nearer than two miles ... so whatever benefit the village has derived from its pipes has been won solely by the skill and industry of the inhabitants.[15]

This skill and industry ensured that the positive reputation of the pipes was enduring and the *Roscommon Journal* proclaimed that 'Knockcroghery ... is a household word throughout the greater part of Connacht ... For nearly all the pipes smoked within a wide radian west of the Shannon are "Knockcrogheries", that is products of the famous pottery at Knockcroghery'.[16] Although Knockcroghery became synonymous with the production of clay pipes, it was an industry that developed in many parts of the country. Pipe-making was recorded in Co. Waterford as early as 1641.[17] The Schools Folklore Collection includes 163 anecdotes referring to clay pipes from twenty-one of the twenty-six counties.[18] The clay pipe, or *dúidín* as it was more colloquially known, was synonymous with Irish wakes and funeral traditions, and was generally viewed as the pipe of the common man. At a wake, as many as a couple of dozen *dúidíns* were filled with complementary tobacco for mourners and sympathizers. Neighbours and friends gathered, and upon viewing the corpse would raise the pipe while stating 'Lord have mercy' [on the soul of the deceased]. This in turn led to the pipe also being known as the 'Lord ha' mercy'. In the spring of 1921, just a few months before the burning of the village, the folklorist Seán Ó Súilleabháin attended a wake at Ballina in Co. Mayo and later recalled:

> As we knew the people of the house, we shook their hands and sympathised with them in their sorrow ... Room was made for us in the corner of the kitchen and a clay pipe, filled with tobacco, was handed to each of us. We accepted the pipes, although none of us was at the stage of using them, and said

the customary prayer, 'May God have mercy on the souls of the dead'. We attempted to 'redden' the pipes, out of respect for the deceased, but only in a half-hearted way.[19]

The production of clay pipes at Knockcroghery was well established by the early nineteenth century and was attributed, as Weld notes, to 'the accidental settlement of a man acquainted with the process from whom others gradually learned the art and mystery'.[20] The earliest record of a known pipe-maker in Knockcroghery appears in the 1749 census of Elphin where Thomas Buckley, a Protestant, resided with his five children.[21] Throughout the eighteenth and nineteenth centuries, the manufactory of clay pipes at Knockcroghery was carried out in small-scale, family owned workshops with no more than eight kilns evident in the mid-nineteenth century.[22] Mulvihill suggests that there were only seven factories in Knockcroghery by the 1890s. Despite this, these seven factories employed about sixty people or approximately 25 per cent of the village's population.

The pipes themselves had a short stem and a small bole. Once sourced, the clay was made into small cakes by hand and left in a warm place – usually by the fire in the family kitchen – to dry. Once the clay was sufficiently dry, it was broken down into a powder. Water was added and the clay prepared for use by rolling and dividing it into smaller portions for moulding. A wire was passed through the stem before being placed in a specially designed mould where the clay was then compressed.[23] The bole of the pipe was formed using a punch, which forced the clay out of the bole creating the cavity into which the tobacco was placed. This process could be completed relatively quickly, and a good pipe maker could produce about 150 pipes in an hour. As Weld concluded, 'A moulder who is moderately steady to his work can turn out from seven to eight groce (*sic*) in a day ... but more might be done with exertion'.[24] The pipes were then 'finished', packaged and prepared for distribution through either the local railway station, or by pedlars who travelled around to fairs and markets selling the produce for less than a halfpenny.[25] Writing about the pipes, the *Roscommon Journal* surmized: 'Then, as now, tinkers wives and other hawkers carried the pipes around the country from fair to fair and the quality of the goods quickly established their reputation in the homes of the west'.[26] Each pipe bore the name of the manufacturer and usually some type of embellishment or logo promoting a political cause or a decorative spiral design, for example.

THE PEOPLE

For families like the Cunnanes or Curleys, who the *Roscommon Herald* noted made a yearly profit of £496 as pipe manufacturers, clay-pipe production was the main source of income for the family.[27] Census data for 1901 and 1911 confirms that multiple family members were involved in the process.[28] While the census returns for the area defined as Scregg DED for the years 1901 and 1911 are useful in building a profile of the local community, some pages are notably missing thus making the record incomplete. Despite this, it is clear from the census data that pipe making was an integral part of the local economy. In 1901 eight family names, representing eleven individual households, were engaged in pipe production. These included well-known pipe producers such as Andrew Curley and his son PJ, and also Martin Cunnane and his two teenage children, Mary (17) and Patrick (15), who worked as a pipe finisher and a pipe maker respectively. Less well-known manufacturers such as brothers Pat and John Glennon, as well as the 36-year-old Patrick Dowd and 80-year-old John Lyons were also engaged in the industry.[29] The age profile of the moulders, ranging from 15 to 80 years of age, is striking and highlights how dependant the local economy was on pipe production. Although women, with the exception of Elizabeth Cunnane, were not recorded as pipe makers, they were clearly actively involved in the business as well. Bridget FitzGerald and Elizabeth Cunnane's sister, Bridget, were recorded as pipe finishers.[30] In 1901, twenty people expressly stated that their occupation was in the clay-pipe production process. Another four pipe makers, Bernard FitzGerald, Peter Gavin and John and Patrick Tierney, were recorded in the townland of Creggan in Mote DED, which was situated to the north of the village. Despite the fact that only some family members clearly stated their occupations as being associated with pipe production, it is exceedingly likely that everyone in the household was involved to some degree in the process. Therefore, the actual importance of the industry to these families is significantly more than the census returns suggest.

By 1911, the number recorded as working in clay-pipe production in Scregg DED had declined by a staggering 50 per cent. Names such as Treacy and Dowd were no longer working in the trade and young men such as Michael Quigley, who in 1901 was recorded as a pipe maker and carter, was now engaged in agricultural activities.[31] Of those enumerated in Creggan DED, Bernard FitzGerald and Peter Gavin were still working in the industry, as were the Tierneys and a new pipe producer named Patrick Comer.[32] However, it is clear that the industry was in decline. By 1910, local clay deposits had been fully exploited and raw materials for the pipes had to be imported from England.[33] This, coupled with a failure to modernize production in general, meant that it was increasingly difficult to support a family on pipe production alone.[34] As the decade progressed, and the First World War ended, the industry was further threatened by new, more fashionable ways of consuming tobacco, specifically in the form of the cigarette. Moreover, emigration from rural Ireland continued to rise thereby compromising the viability of small-scale industries such as clay-pipe manufacturing.

THE COMMUNITY

Aside from pipe production but due, partially at least, to its success, the village also boasted a number of other commercial enterprises. By 1921, there were at least three shops: Jackson's; John S. Murray's and Denis O'Brien's, which had recently opened a 'general drapery and millinery warehouse'.[35] A number of licensed premises including the Widow Murray's, Jackson's and O'Brien's were also in operation and these no doubt enlivened social opportunities in the area. Jackson's was especially well known for holding dances. In his diaries for 1920, Benjamin Greene of Hill House, Lecarrow, recorded two dances in particular at the beginning of 1920, one of which was held in mid-January and the other at the end of February. The January event was attended by twenty-six people according to Greene and his children did not return until 6.30 the following morning.[36]

Agriculture was the other main economic focus of the community. In both the 1901 and 1911 census returns, farming or farm-related activity was a prominent source of employment. Knockcroghery was close to both Roscommon and Athlone towns and so farmers were regularly able to benefit from competitive markets for their livestock and other agricultural produce. The thrice-yearly fairs in the village were also an important component of the local economy, particularly for the sale of sheep, while also providing a social outlet for the community. Greene recorded trading both pigs and sheep at the fairs. At the pig fair in January 1920, he noted, 'We went to the fair in Knockcroghery with seven fat pigs, we got £104 for them'.[37] The following September there was an account of James, his son, buying '40 lambs at from £4 to £4 10/-'.[38]

As well as the fair, a ploughing match was held annually at Ballymurray, just north of the village, and other ploughing matches were held around the parish. Greene records attending 'a ploughing match in Jack Gately's of Killighan' on 4 March 1920 and social activities linked with agriculture were popular in the community.[39] Sporting activities were common and in July 1920 an article appeared in the *Westmeath Independent* promoting a sports day with events including 'Athletics and cycling, jumping and weight throwing'. The afternoon concluded with a football tournament.[40] The GAA also had a very visible presence and local newspapers regularly published fixtures in which Knockcroghery was listed.[41] In 1914, a Ladies' Hurling Club Picnic was held at Rinn Duin Castle in the south of the parish where 'the large company which consisted of about 100' spent the day 'dancing, boating and singing'.[42] A social gathering by the shores of Lough Ree seemed a popular way to spend a Sunday afternoon as Greene also records a picnic that was organized by the Revd Mr Humphries, which took place at Gailey Bay in July 1920. About twenty people were in attendance, he notes.[43] Ostensibly, the people of Knockcroghery seemed, in many ways, to continue with their everyday lives; yet this existence was in the context of an increasingly belligerent War of Independence, a war that, up to the summer of 1920 at least, seemed to have had very little impact on the village. As 1920 drew to a close, however, this 'national' war had progressively more local repercussions.

2. The war

As the second decade of the twentieth century progressed, the diverse range of political opinion that existed nationally was replicated in Knockcroghery and emerging national trends were increasingly evident in the locality. The complexity of political discourse generated extensive discussion and participation in the locality and in 1916 Fr Kelly, the Catholic parish priest, had advocated for the re-establishment of a branch of the United Irish League. A public meeting followed, after which a committee was formed with Kelly acting as president.[1] By 1918, a Sinn Féin club had also been established in the village and representatives, along with counterparts from other clubs in south Roscommon, attended a meeting at Harrison Hall in Roscommon town with the aim of forming a Sinn Féin executive for south Roscommon.[2]

THE LOCALITY

Meanwhile, during the summer of the previous year, 1917, the Knockcroghery company of the Irish Volunteers was established with twelve members.[3] Patrick Kelly became the company's first captain and John Brehony, the first lieutenant.[4] Two other companies, the St John's company and the Rahara company, were formed in the parish in the same year.[5] Each company formed part of the 4th Battalion, South Roscommon Brigade, 2nd Western Division and were active in a number of operations throughout the War of Independence. Parades were held regularly on Tuesday and Thursday evenings at which there was a 'roll call, collecting of dues ... studying maps ... [and] periods of one to two hours drill'.[6] In April 1920 the Knockcroghery company participated in the burning of the RIC barracks at Lecarrow (fig. 1), 5km to the south, at which 'all officers and men were present'. In his diary, Benjamin Greene noted that the burning of Lecarrow barracks was not an isolated attack, writing: 'Monday 5 April: Yesterday was a fine day for Easter Sunday, but great harm was done throughout Ireland. Sixty barracks were burned to the ground that were closed, Lecarrow barracks was burned to the ground and four others in the Co. Roscommon'.[7] The company was also responsible for providing armed escorts to bank officials as they took large sums of money to fairs at Knockcroghery.[8] It was customary for local branches of the National Bank to open a temporary branch office on fair days to facilitate trading at the fair. However, owning to increasing unrest in south Roscommon, this practice was discontinued, which had a 'menacing' effect on the fair. As the *Offaly Independent* noted, 'A police guard was not considered desirable and the difficulty was overcome by a number of young men of the locality voluntarily undertaking to guard the [bank] manager and the money', which amounted to approximately £30,000.[9] The Sinn Féin hall was used as the impromptu bank and 'while the bank manager was in occupation, the young men remained on guard and they escorted him safely to Roscommon in the evening'.[10] According to the activity log of the Knockcroghery company, this happened on three occasions and involved six members of the company.[11] Police activity was also evident in the area and on 21 May 1920, Benjamin Greene nonchalantly recorded in his diary that 'The police were taking up guns. We had to give ours', while later in the year, in late November, he noted that 'The Black and Tans came up today to fix their motor lorry', evidence perhaps that the ongoing war became integrated into people's everyday lives.[12]

One of the most high-profile operations undertaken by the Knockcroghery company was the assassination of RIC Constable William J. Potter, a policeman from Castlebar, who was fatally wounded on 26 August 1920. Potter was based at Kiltoom station, about halfway between Knockcroghery and Athlone, and was returning from Roscommon after delivering a letter with fellow policeman Constable Michael McMahon. McMahon recalled that 'two men rushed out from the road-side and fired at us'.[13] Four shots were fired, one of which fatally wounded Potter. McMahon managed to escape to safety, 'firing four shots over his left shoulder' in defence.[14] He also recalled seeing 'six persons where [they] were ambushed', a claim confirmed by the activity log of the Knockcroghery company.[15] Greene, in his diary, noted that Potter 'was shot at 2 o'clock this morning'.[16] The jury at Potter's inquest concluded that Constable

Potter 'met his death at Knockcroghery from a bullet wound inflicted by some person unknown'.[17] This operation, however, was an opportune attack by the Knockcroghery company and had not been sanctioned by either the battalion or the brigade officers. In his BMH witness statement, Matthew Davis, from the neighbouring parish of Kilteevan and quartermaster of the South Roscommon Brigade, claimed that Potter was in fact an IRA informant and had been 'in touch with Collins and was supplying information to him'.[18]

It is likely that Potter was indeed an informant as it subsequently emerged that other RIC men in Kiltoom station were sympathetic to the IRA cause. The week before Potter's assassination, Brian Lenihan, the officer commanding of the Kiltoom company, had been contacted by Sergeant Galligan of Kiltoom station, via the local Catholic priest. Galligan was open to handing over the barracks and its accompanying armament to the local IRA if 'a serious attack on it [the station] was made by the IRA ... to cover up or cloak from his superiors his actions in the affair'.[19] According to Thomas Kelly, O/C of the 4th Battalion, South Roscommon Brigade, 'he also indicated that one or two of the constables was willing to help the IRA in the capture of the place'.[20] However, Lenihan was suspicious of Galligan's motivations and, fearing subterfuge, he was slow to engage with Galligan. After much effort, a meeting between Lenihan and Galligan was organized at the priest's house in Curraghboy (fig. 1) for Sunday 31 August 1920, four days after the assassination of Potter. The meeting never took place, however, as the Kiltoom RIC barracks was closed the previous Friday – the day after and as a direct result of Potter's murder. Kelly recalls that this was indeed a missed opportunity as there were at least fourteen men stationed at Kiltoom and the acquisition of the armament there would have represented a significant coup for the South Roscommon Brigade. Thus, the shooting of Potter by members of the Knockcroghery company, and its unintended consequences highlight how the lack of communication, and indeed indiscipline, both between and within local IRA companies, at times impeded the objectives of the brigade in more substantial ways.

In the days and weeks after Potter's murder, tensions in the greater Athlone, Kiltoom and Knockcroghery areas increased exponentially. A curfew was imposed on the town of Athlone in response to the heightened tensions and Fr Columba, a Franciscan friar in the town, called for 'patience and fortitude', advising young men to 'keep off the streets at night'.[21] A fortnight after Potter's murder, the *Westmeath Independent* reported that McMahon had resigned from the RIC and 'two other constables have also resigned in Kiltoom station'.[22] Notably, the paper overlooked the fact that the station had been terminated in the interim.

THE AUXILIARIES ARRIVE

By September 1920 it had become increasingly apparent that the RIC needed reinforcements, not only in the greater Roscommon, Westmeath and Longford area, but across the country as a whole. To this end, the Auxiliary division of the RIC was formed and on the evening of 16 October 1920, a group of these troops arrived at Victoria Barracks in Athlone (fig. 1). The rationale behind the introduction of the Auxiliary Division was to 'stiffen the RIC by the infusion of companies composed of men of experience and proved capability'.[23] In British military parlance, Knockcroghery formed part of the 5th Division and was situated a mere 12km from Victoria Barracks, one of the most significant military bases in the Midlands. Athlone was the headquarters of the 13th Infantry, 1st Division, and covered counties Westmeath, Longford, Roscommon, Galway, Mayo and south Leitrim. The 5th Division in Athlone consisted predominantly of three infantry battalions and one cavalry regiment but comprised support staff in the form of the RASC and RAMC among others. An enumeration of troops in the 5th Division based in Athlone on 16 July 1921, less than a week after the truce had been agreed, recorded that there was a total of 43 officers and 869 soldiers of other ranks across infantry, cavalry, RASC, RAMC, RE and others.[24] Until his death on 20 June 1921, Colonel-Commandant Thomas Stanton Lambert was the general officer commanding for all of these troops, a position which he had been appointed to in 1919. Lambert was born in London in 1871 and was the son of a vicar. He was commissioned in the East Lancashire Regiment and served in India before the First World War. In 1914, he was promoted to the rank of major and commanded troops at Contalmaison, La Sars and Menin Road, and was well respected in military circles.

The arrival of these auxiliary troops on that Saturday evening in October 1920 signalled the beginning of the most intense phase of the War of Independence in the region. The *Westmeath Independent* noted that 'during the latter days of the previous week ... large quantities of stores and munitions of war [and] troops passing and repassing in lorries forming an almost constant procession through the streets' was evident in the town.[25] Over the course of the next nine months, raids, ambushes, attacks and reprisals were more prevalent as both sides became entrenched in an increasingly provocative guerrilla war.[26] Just hours after their arrival, the *Westmeath Independent* termed Athlone a 'veritable hell' from 'midnight to morning' as during the night the Athlone printing works was partially burned and there were a number of raids on homes in Main Street and High Street.[27] The following morning 'a state of great excitement prevailed' as a large boat owned by J.J. Coen, justice of the peace, was commandeered and a while later an extemporaneous retaliation by Coosan IRA resulted in 'continuous machine-gun and rifle fire from the direction of Lough Ree [which] was distinctly audible in the town'.[28] Upon their return, it transpired that two officers and three soldiers had been wounded.[29] Lambert recorded in the official report that:

> On 17 October 1920 at 7.30 in the morning, 20 officers and soldiers of the 13th Inf. departed Victoria Barracks with orders to commandeer two boats and search a number of islands on L Ree as there was believed to be arms stored on them. Only one boat was requisitioned, a boat belonging to Mr Coen, and ultimately the search on the islands was unsuccessful. Upon their return, the boat was fired on by rebels as it passed Athlone Yacht Club hut. Major Adams received a severe gunshot wound to the left shoulder. It was estimated that as many as 150 IRA were present. The boat was hit about 40 times.[30]

Pointedly, only twenty-nine men were identified in the Athlone Brigade activity report as having taken part in the ambush.[31] Lambert later noted that 'certain leading townspeople are anxious that I should receive a deputation but so far I have declined'.[32] As the end of October 1920 approached, tensions between both sides were undoubtedly fraught.

Attacks and reprisals on both sides continued to escalate during the winter of 1921 as IRA companies in south Roscommon, Longford and Westmeath continued their agitation. In her chronology of the War of Independence in Co. Roscommon, Hegarty-Thorne records a number of incidents in the early part of the year that helped sustain the rebel effort in the region.[33] In early January, the 3rd Battalion, South Roscommon Brigade attempted an ambush of RIC men at Lanesboro, which was followed a few weeks later by an unofficial operation of the Athlone flying column at Cornafulla, to the west of Athlone on the Ballinasloe Road.[34] The leader of the column, James Tormey, was killed in the attack, which was orchestrated in retribution for the assassination of his brother, Joseph, at Ballykinlar internment camp a fortnight earlier. Throughout the month of February, there was a series of British military raids on Strokestown in pursuit of rebels and their illegally acquired arms, possibly acting on intelligence about a potential ambush in the area which ultimately manifested itself as the Scramogue ambush a month later. These raids resulted in the arrest of almost 200 people on 20 February.[35]

For the most part, large-scale operations by the IRA in the region were relatively few, but two significant ambushes in north Longford and east Roscommon in February and March 1921, respectively, inadvertently helped to seal the fate of Knockcroghery a few months later. The first of these was the Clonfin ambush between Granard and Ballinalee in north Co. Longford.[36] In late 1920, the North Longford flying column was established and led by the formidable Sean MacEoin.[37] The twenty-one-man-strong company was responsible for a number of attacks on the RIC and British army including a successful ambush on the RIC in Ballinalee in November 1920 and their most important and effective operation at Clonfin on 2 February 1921. This ambush resulted in the death of four members of the ADRIC and caused serious injury to another eight men. MacEoin recalled that his 'decision was to place a mine in the road to blow up the first lorry [of ADRIC men] and at the same time to concentrate all the fire power of one of my sections on the occupants of the second lorry'.[38] After a short battle, the ADRIC surrendered upon incurring a number of casualties and fatalities including Lieutenant

Commander Francis W. Craven, the commanding officer on the day of the ambush. The days and weeks after the Clonfin incident were characterized by retaliations, reprisals and the burning of cottages in the greater Granard area.

After the ambush, MacEoin was a marked man. He continued to lead the North Longford flying column but his actions were closely observed. In early March, a month after the Clonfin attack, MacEoin was in Dublin attending an interview with the Sinn Féin minister for defence, Cathal Brugha. After a subsequent meeting with Michael Collins, MacEoin boarded the train to Longford, where he spent part of the journey conversing with fifteen British soldiers while simultaneously concocting a plan to ambush them in Edgeworthstown when he was reunited with his flying column.[39] As they approached Mullingar, the train became stationary, not on its usual platform, but on a siding. All civilians were ordered off the train for inspection and after being identified by Head Constable Kidd, despite claiming his identity was J.J. Smith from Aughnacliffe, MacEoin was arrested and brought to Mullingar RIC barracks.[40] He was later charged with the murder of DI Thomas McGrath on 7 January 1921 and a date for his trial, 14 June, was arranged.[41] Pointedly, this was seven days before the village of Knockcroghery was burned. While geographically the Clonfin ambush had little effect on events in Knockcroghery, it was nonetheless significant as it was the subsequent arrest of MacEoin that set in train a series of events that led to the burning.

The second regional incident of note that exacerbated antagonisms between both sides during the early spring of 1921 was the Scramogue ambush.[42] This was comparable with the Clonfin ambush in a number of ways. The target was strategically valuable, especially given the paucity of arms and ammunition in Roscommon at the time. Moreover, the movement of the army and RIC was relatively predictable and this paved the way for a well-orchestrated and well-executed attack. This operation was intricately planned and involved cooperation between the 3rd North Roscommon Brigade and the 3rd South Roscommon Brigade. Shortly after 7.30 on the morning of 23 March 1921, the sound of lorries starting their engines in Strokestown could be heard 4km to the east of the town at Scramogue. Although there should have been two Crossley tenders in convoy, on that particular morning, a lone tender carrying a nine-man patrol consisting mainly of men from the 9th Lancers Regiment was met with a volley of shots from the IRA who were commanded on the morning by Pat Madden. On approach, shots were fired at the lorry and the officer commanding the British troops, Captain Roger Peek, a former German POW, was fatally wounded. Oral testimony of the ambush is contradictory, but as well as four fatalities, two of whom were officers, the IRA also commandeered some revolvers, rifles, ammunition and a highly prized Hotchkiss gun.[43] Notably, and perhaps in the hope of saving his life, one of the captured British soldiers showed the IRA how to use the gun, before he was subsequently executed in a nearby bog. Following the ambush, the enquiry conducted by the British army concluded that there was a shortage of vehicles in Strokestown on the morning of 23 March and this meant that the policy of travelling in convoy, in a minimum detachment of two vehicles, was not possible.[44] The Scramogue ambush was one of the most high-profile operations that took place in Roscommon during the War of Independence. Its relevance to Knockcroghery was the acquisition of the Hotchkiss gun, which was, allegedly, to be transported to the village and used in a subsequent attack on British forces later in the year. Just as in the aftermath of the Clonfin ambush, military presence in the greater Strokestown area increased almost immediately. The following day saw the murder of Michael Mullolly, a brother of one of the leaders of the ambush. This was just one in a series of reprisals and retaliations by the British forces which characterized the last days of March 1921.

Despite these high-profile regional engagements, the War of Independence trundled on at a local level as well. In November 1920 two members of the ADRIC raided Miss Jackson's shop in Knockcroghery. Constable John Duffy was an IRA informant stationed predominately in Athlone, but also in Kiltoom and Roscommon during this period and on the night of the sacking recalled witnessing two men, Johnston and Knight, leaving the barracks at around 4.30p.m. They returned later that night with a significant loot recorded by Duffy as being a blanket 'bearing 57/6d. on the tag label' and underneath it 'were three cardboard boxes'. He continued that one of the boxes 'contained cut plug tobacco, the next box contained bar plug tobacco and the third was full of ladies' underwear'. There were also two 'five naggin bottles of whiskey' at the window and wrapped up in another blanket was a further one thousand boxes of polish.[45] On orders from head constable, Duffy searched one of the auxiliaries and as well as two loaded revolvers. Duffy also uncovered 'a lady's gold watch, a silver watch and a gold medal which was initialled "J.J."'.[46] Duffy concluded that the value of the property found on their persons was £40, all of which had been taken from the Jackson sisters, or the 'Misses Jackson' as they were known locally, who were shopkeepers in Knockcroghery.[47] A case was later taken against the two men, and both were sentenced to three years in Brixton prison for the offence.

A few weeks later, the Knockcroghery company was involved in an attempted attack on the British military in the village in January 1921, as well as a subsequent attempted attack at Scrine to the west of the village. Thereafter, the RIC raided Knockcroghery in early March and this was followed two weeks later, on 17 March (St Patrick's Day), by further RIC raids in Rahara. On 11 April, a prominent member of the Knockcroghery company was arrested and interned. The Knockcroghery company was also actively involved in the making of munitions for the battalion. Thomas Kelly recalled that 'during the early part of 1921 a large amount of buckshot was made in the battalion area' primarily as a result of the 'large amount of gelignite from the railway quarries at Lecarrow'.[48] As well as buckshot for shotgun cartridges, bombs and grenades were also fashioned from tin cans, gelignite and a powder-trail fuse.[49] Perhaps the most significant event in the parish in 1921, before the burning in late June, was the murder of a 67-year-old blacksmith at Carnagh, St John's on 1 June. Patrick Coyle, from Bredagh, Kiltoom, was at the home of Hubert Murphy tending to a horse, when, as the *Irish Independent* reported, 'a police patrol serving jurors' summons' noticed men running away from the house as the patrol approached.[50] When the men failed to stop after being ordered to, an altercation occurred in which one constable was wounded and the blacksmith was shot. Coyle died soon after as a result of his wound. The paper continues that Coyle 'had no connection with politics' and that the deceased was 'known as an inoffensive man'.[51] The subsequent inquiry concluded that Coyle's death was as a result of involuntary manslaughter.[52]

At this stage in the war, two things were becoming increasingly apparent. First, it seemed that the IRA in the greater Roscommon-

Westmeath area was dominating the local guerrilla war, despite their lack of resources and experience compared with their adversaries. Second, their British opponents were increasingly frustrated and as the War Office nonchalantly recorded

> The military situation in the country from May [1921] onwards showed little change in the methods employed by the rebels. Attacks on a large scale were infrequent but minor outrages such as raids on mails [and] holding up of trains conveying military stores ... continued.

These minor attacks were becoming more frequent and 'during the Whitsuntide weekend (14–15 May), no less than 11 outrages involving murder took place'.[53] In an attempt to counteract this IRA activity, the army embarked on a series of 'drives' throughout May and early June 1921. They were conducted by cavalry regiments with the intention of interrogating 'every male civilian ... and all who could be identified as members of the IRA were to be detained and houses searched for arms'.[54] The success of these raids was questionable and by far a more effective intervention was the restrictions placed on telegraph facilities to counteract increasingly violent activity from the rebels including the aforementioned murders and attacks on troop trains.

In general terms, the War Office noted that the British army faced a number of difficulties in effectively dealing with the rebels. There was a lack of internment camps in Ireland, despite the fact that by June 1921 more than four thousand members of the IRA were interned. The other problem identified by the general staff was the lack of ships to patrol the coast and impede the illegal importation of arms.[55] These, and a number of other regional factors, had negatively impacted the morale of the troops by the early summer of 1921. In May, General Macready, the commander-in-chief of British forces in Ireland, submitted two memoranda to the chief of the imperial general staff. The first considered the moral and physical state of the army and stated that the 'atmosphere' under which the troops were serving could not be appreciated by anybody outside of Ireland.[56] This was followed by a particularly dubious claim attesting that 'Although the murder of officers and men was a daily occurrence, there had been during the last few months, not a single instance of retaliation'. However, he continued by warning that 'if pressed too far by the campaign of outrage and murder against them, there might [...] be cases where they would take the law into their own hands'.[57] The burning of Knockcroghery just a few short weeks later would appear to be a case in point and a candid manifestation of their frustration.

THE ASSASSINATION OF GENERAL LAMBERT

On the day before his assassination, Lambert had invoked Regulation 13 of the Restoration of Order in Ireland Regulations (ROIR) and imposed a curfew on the urban district of Athlone from 2200 hours until 0500 hours, as a result of the murder of an RIC constable in Kilbeggan and a number of outrages throughout Westmeath in the previous weeks.[58] The trial and subsequent sentencing to death of Sean MacEoin further impassioned IRA virulence in the region and, in the days after the trial, the Athlone Brigade planned an operation in which they intended to take arms from General Lambert as he returned from a tennis party at Killinure House.[59] Thomas Costello, O/C of the Athlone Brigade, recorded: 'Captain Elliot of the Tubberclare company of Volunteers was instructed to round up this party and if they carried arms to disarm them. Elliot laid an ambush for the party on the road out to Midges'.[60] Although the incident is recorded in the activity report for the Athlone Brigade, the detail provided is practical but scant. There is no account of the ambush and the only information provided in the log are the names of the men involved.[61] Nonetheless, an examination of Bureau of Military History witness statements as well as newspapers indicate that between 7.15p.m. and 7.30p.m. on 20 June 1921, General Lambert, his wife, Geraldine, and their companions Colonel and Mrs Challoner and Challoner's niece, Ms Katie Elsie Arthurs, were travelling towards Athlone having attended a tennis party at Killinure House that afternoon. The *Freeman's Journal* notes that the 'occupants of the car were called to a halt by six armed civilians' as it approached Harmony Hall at Benown near Glasson.[62] Instead of halting, Mrs Lambert, the driver of the car, accelerated after which shots were fired. Mrs Challoner, the front-seat passenger, received minor injuries to her face from gunshot pellets, while General Lambert, who was sitting in the rear of the car, was shot in the neck.[63] Mrs Lambert proceeded to the military hospital in Victoria Barracks, but General Lambert was pronounced dead at 9p.m. and within a few hours the village of Knockcroghery was ablaze.

3. The burning

Lambert was held in high esteem by his men and news of his death spread quickly around the barracks and further afield. According to the official report compiled by the War Office, initial intelligence uncovered after Lambert's murder 'pointed to the fact that the ambushers were about fourteen in number and came from a district on the western and opposite side of Lough Ree'.[1] This was confirmed by an the article published in the *Irish Times* the day after the burning, which stated: 'the men that were in the armed attack at Benown on Monday were seen crossing the fields towards Lough Ree, by which it is believed they escaped in boats to the Connaught shore'.[2] By a coincidence of geography, Knockcroghery was the closest and most developed settlement north of Athlone on the western shore of the lake and so it was presumed that the Knockcroghery company had been involved in the ambush and subsequent murder of Lambert.

In the daily briefing of police reports submitted by the RIC to the under-secretary at Dublin Castle on 22 June 1921, a two-line summary of the events in Knockcroghery the previous night were outlined. The report read: 'Co. Roscommon. In the early hours of 21 June 1921, fifteen houses in the village of Knockcroghery were maliciously burned and destroyed'.[3] The lack of information is telling, especially when compared with the report received the previous day outlining the murder of General Lambert. Nonetheless, although accounts of the burning vary slightly, a broad narrative can be constructed thus: Between 1a.m. and 1.30a.m. on the night of 20–21 June 1921, two military lorries carrying approximately fifteen armed, disguised and drunken men in civilian clothing arrived in the village from the Athlone direction. They parked on the southern end of the village and proceeded northwards, setting a number of homes on fire while simultaneously firing revolvers and threatening the residents of the village. The *Irish Independent* reported that 'during the burning there were constant fusillades of rifle and revolver firing. Terrified people rushed out of their homes and escaped through the fields'.[4] Of the nineteen homes targeted on the night, fifteen were destroyed in the attack while three houses and the presbytery escaped serious damage. The paper continued: 'The 3 houses untouched are those of John Murray, Widow Murray and Murtaghs'.[5] Residents of the village fled into the neighbouring countryside in their night attire, predominantly in the direction of Hangman's hill to the north-east, and gradually made their way to the southern end of the village where 'subsequently, children and aged persons were taken into the presbytery ... and the Revd Mr Humphries's rectory where they were kindly treated'.[6] The following day the *Evening Herald* glibly noted that 'The old-fashioned village of Knockcroghery, Co. Roscommon, [is] the latest victim of the petrol tin and flaming torch' while the *Freeman's Journal* added that 'The village presents a shocking appearance being a mass of smouldering ruins with the former occupants homeless and destitute'.[7]

THE RESIDENTS

The *Irish Independent* claimed that the population of the village in 1921 was ninety-four.[8] Of these, four residents were under the age of one on the night of the burning.[9] At the time of the burning there were still two significant pipe factories in the village. One of those belonged to Patrick Curley whose house was the first to be targeted. As part of Curley's compensation hearing, the *Roscommon Herald* reported his experience of that night, noting:

> The door was burst in and two men, apparently officers entered. Without getting time to dress he was put out at the point of a revolver, the floor was sprinkled with petrol and the house set on fire. He took to the fields and his children, who were practically naked were taken in by the Rector, Rev. Mr Humphries ... who provided them with clothing ... The witness informed Mr Hannon [solicitor] that he had been advanced some money by the White Cross.[10]

In various reports and recollections of the night of the burning, as well as in local lore, the kindness shown to the residents by the

rector, Revd Mr Humphries, was both altruistic and benevolent.[11]
The *Roscommon Herald* noted the Revd Mr Humphries and his wife
'gave them every assistance' and the community were 'sincerely
grateful to them for their truly Christian acts'.[12] Two of the solicitors
representing the residents of the village at a subsequent compensation
hearing, Mr McSharry and Mr Neilan, also expressed their desire to
have the record show the gratitude that the residents of the village
had for Revd Humphries and his wife. Such was the Humphries'
contribution to the community on the night that the *Freeman's Journal*
was moved to write the following in an editorial a few months after
the burning:

> Out of the smoke of Knockcroghery emerges one figure that
> we trust may be a symbol of the future. The good Samaritans
> of Knockcroghery that helped to shelter and shield the naked
> infants and houseless women of Knockcroghery were the
> Protestant rector and his wife. Revd Mr Humphries and
> Mrs Humphries have done more by their Christianity on this
> occasion for the cause of goodwill and mutual toleration …
> his fine and courageous Christianity will be remembered in
> Connacht long after the mercenary mutilators and incendiaries
> have ceased – even to be an evil memory.[13]

Local stories abound about the number of Knockcroghery men
that could be seen in clergymen's garb in the days after the burning,
but there seems to be at least some truth to these tales as the *Irish
Independent* noted two days after the burning that 'Others were
afforded shelter in the presbytery and rectory, many of the male
refugees having been supplied with clothes by both clergymen'.[14]

In the two years before the burning, Revd Mr Humphries and
Fr Bartley Kelly, the Catholic parish priest in Knockcroghery,
had developed a unique friendship that nurtured an environment
of mutual toleration and respect within the community. Their
collaborative spirit in the days after the burning ensured that the
community was clothed, sheltered and fed, and also resulted in aid
arriving in the village from the White Cross within a number of
weeks. For his part, Fr Kelly also had a traumatic experience on the
night. The *Roscommon Herald* recorded that

the occupants [of the lorries which had parked near the presbytery] got out and went in the direction of Knockcroghery and ... some time after [the] front door was burst in and one of the men came up to him. He could identify him as a military officer he had often seen in mufti [plain clothes] in Athlone. The officer ordered him out and, when he refused to go, he fired two shots over his head ... He eventually got out of a back window and concealed himself in a field of oats.[15]

The *Irish Independent* claimed that 'armed men rushed up to his bedroom and ordered him to get out'. Kelly refused, but after the perpetrators 'sprinkl[ed] petrol over the furniture, he went through the bedroom window and dropped 12ft on to a shed and then to the ground'.[16] Although the attackers did manage to set the presbytery, which had only been built the previous decade, on fire, the quick thinking of women like Jenny Quigley helped to extinguish the fire with sand and water.[17] However, despite this, Kelly's extensive library, which included a number of rare volumes, was destroyed.[18]

One of the residents in the village on the night of the burning was 4-year-old Jimmy Murray, a son of John S. Murray and his wife, Susan, whose house suffered only minimal damage on the night. In an interview published in 2003, Jimmy recalled the night of the burning. He started by describing Knockcroghery as a 'village of thatched houses, except for a couple that had slate roofs. Nearly all were one-storey buildings' and most, except for two, were on one side of the street.[19] He also noted that the summer of 1921 was warm, resulting in highly flammable thatch. Thus, all the perpetrators had to do was 'sprinkle petrol and a match and away they went'.[20] Speaking about his own family's experience of the fire, Murray remembered:

> The house I lived in was one of the houses that wasn't burned that night, simply because it was a three-storey slated house and it was impossible for them to climb on the roof to set it on fire. However, they attempted to set the back door of the shop alight, but my father with the help of some others managed to quench it before it caught hold.[21]

Under the same roof as John S. Murray's shop was the post office, which was operated by Mrs Owens. On the night of the burning, Charlie Owens, the local schoolteacher, and husband of the postmistress, confronted the attackers and argued that the post office was a government building and that it would be unwise to cause any damage to it. His reasoning was effective and the entire structure which included Murray's shop and the post office remained intact, aside from some fire damage to the back door of the shop.[22] The second house to avoid destruction on the night of the burning was Murtaghs'. Little is known about the family as they were relatively new to the area, not having been enumerated in the 1911 census. However, on the night of the burning there was a one-month-old baby in the house.[23] Their home also survived because of its slated roof.

Of the many anecdotes that survive from that night, it is perhaps the bravery of the Widow Murray that is the most remarkable. As Jimmy Murray recalled, 'Mrs Murray was a widow with six young children and she came out on the street that morning with the six children around her and pleaded for mercy. Well as bad as they were, they didn't burn her house and they let her go'.[24] In the years before the burning, Mrs Murray had lost her husband and youngest child (an eight-month-old daughter) to tuberculosis and she was left with taking care of her family as well as the business, a licensed premises.[25] However, on that night she held firm and stated her case to the assailants. Jimmy Murray continued that

> Every other house in the village was burned to the ground, though some families managed to save a room or two where they lived afterwards ... Perhaps people at the Roscommon end of the village fared a little better as they had a few minutes grace while the Tans were moving down the street.[26]

THE DAYS AFTER THE BURNING

News of the burning spread almost as quickly as the flames themselves. The following morning reports of the sacking had reached the national newspapers. The burning of the village was mentioned in the context of Lambert's killing and the kidnapping of the earl of Bandon, which had taken place the previous day. By Wednesday 22 June reports of the burning were beginning to appear in the international press. The *Daily Mirror*, published in London, as well as regional newspapers in Birmingham and Sheffield each carried a generic, albeit misinformed press telegram about the burning.[27] By Thursday, the events in Knockcroghery had made the front page of the *Indiana Daily Times* and the attack was also reported in the *New York Times*. In Australia, it was included alongside a discussion on the Northern Irish parliament in the *Sydney Morning Herald*.[28] However, despite the international coverage, the local newspapers made a sobering decision to forego extensive reporting on the events in Knockcroghery when their editions were published the following Saturday. It is likely that this was an instinctual attempt at self-protection as no doubt they were cognizant of the fate that befell the Athlone Printing Works the previous October.

Aside from the international press, the matter was also raised in the House of Commons by the leader of the significantly diminished Irish Parliamentary Party, Joseph Devlin, on 23 June 1921. Devlin asked the chief secretary of Ireland if he was aware of the burning of the village, and if so could he elaborate on the detail of the event. In his absence, Denis Henry, the attorney general for Ireland, answered by acknowledging the burning had taken place and summarized the police report published in the hours after the burning. Devlin, in an attempt to 'try and get at the truth about something in Ireland', called upon Henry to 'take steps to have some impartial tribunal appointed to inquire into this wholesale destruction of an Irish village'.[29] Henry countered by stating that the perpetrators must be ascertained before 'there can be any question of an inquiry'. Arguably both men knew that the perpetrators would not, at any point in the investigation, be formally identified and so the debate moved on to a discussion about the League of Nations.

Back in Knockcroghery, the majority of homes had been lost and most people were unable to save any of their properties. There were now fifteen destitute families with very few personal belongings. Most of the families had no choice but to leave the village in the immediate aftermath of the fires. Some stayed with relatives, and others were offered homes by members of the community until the compensation claims were heard and their homes in the village were rebuilt. Others still were able to salvage a room or two of their homes and so they remained in the village. Michael Lyons, remembers hearing from his own father Pat, who was 14 on the night of the burning, that he 'slept in a horse's cart for a couple of years'.[30] Jimmy Murray captured the dispersion of the village residents in the days after the fire as follows:

> The O'Briens and the Cunnanes went to Shragh. The cottages there were newly built at the time. Two of them were occupied by two elderly bachelors called Ned Bentley and Harry Treacy. I don't know where they stayed, but they gave their houses to the O'Briens and the Cunnanes. P.J. Curley's [family] went to live over in Gailey ... That was a big house and it was unoccupied at the time – it was owned by a Robert Payne who owned all the land around there. The Lyons and the FitzGeralds had two fine big outhouses out the back and they converted them into living quarters until the new houses were built. William Curley's [family] at the end of the street went up to Cornamart to live with an uncle, John Thewlis. The Jacksons owned the two houses on the other side of the street and, as far as I remember, they saved part of one and lived there. The Gordans as well managed to save at least one room and they had to make do with that until the new houses were built.[31]

In economic terms, the village was devastated. Although the demand for clay pipes had been in decline for almost a decade, they were nonetheless still very popular in rural Ireland. The two primary clay-pipe factories in the village had been destroyed in the fires and with them the industry virtually disappeared. Emigration became a more salient feature of life for the younger members of the village, while those who stayed behind turned to agriculture as a means of providing for their families. A combination of resilience and necessity ensured that within a short time the village fairs were re-established. Less than six months after the burning, in January and February 1922, Benjamin Greene recorded that he had attended pig fairs in the village, noting that 'two fat pigs' were bought for £19 5s. at the latter.[32] A few months later, in July, Greene also documented a sports day being held in the village at which 'about 200 attended' and the following September he enjoyed three hours of 'good sport' and entertainment at the circus which had visited the village.[33]

Politically, however, the aftermath of the burning was significantly more complex. Although within three weeks of the burning of Knockcroghery a truce had been agreed in the War of Independence, the interim was characterized, at a local level, by a high-profile funeral and continued attacks and reprisals.

4. The aftermath

On the morning of 21 June 1921, as a smoky haze hung over the smouldering village of Knockcroghery and General Lambert's widow, Geraldine, began making arrangements for her husband's funeral, a military inquiry was underway investigating the circumstances surrounding Lambert's death. At the end of the proceedings, the enquiry found that General Lambert had died from

> shock and haemorrhage, caused by wounds from [a] gunshot, fired by masked and armed men, such persons being guilty of murder and being in a prepared ambush are rebels and are of those acting against the crown.[1]

As news of Lambert's fate reverberated around the town there was widespread shock. The *Freeman's Journal* reported that the 'deceased was held in high esteem by the people of Athlone. All classes … deplore the loss of a kindly disposed and popular gentleman'.[2] Whether the people of Athlone did hold Lambert in 'high esteem' or not is questionable, but nonetheless businesses in the town ceased trading the following day as a mark of respect. Some newspapers reported that shops and businesses were ordered to close after an unsigned handwritten notice was posted on the door of the post office but, as it was unofficial act, the sign was subsequently removed.[3] As well as shops and businesses closing, a sitting of the Athlone petty sessions scheduled for the day after the murder was also suspended.[4] On the morning of the funeral itself, however, there was an official order published requesting that all shops and offices cease trading between 9a.m. and noon though, as the *Irish Independent* noted, 'shops and factories were already closed'.[5] It seems likely that these local businesses were closed out of a fear of the repercussions should they open, rather than out of respect, as suggested by many of the newspapers.

As the week progressed, the national newspapers continued to report on Lambert's untimely death and noted how 'Mrs Lambert, who is prostrate with grief, has received many messages of sympathy'.[6] By Thursday, the funeral had been organized and detailed coverage was again evident in several national titles. Lambert's remains were removed to St Peter's Protestant church where they were received by the Revd Mr Anderson.[7] The cortege left the military hospital in Victoria Barracks (fig. 1) and was carried by six sergeants from the 1st Leicestershire Regiment, after which men from the RASC, Dragoons, RE and RIC followed. Civilian employees at the military barracks and the general public were also present. The funeral service took place on Thursday afternoon and was attended by a large crowd including Lambert's two sons, Edwin, who was 20 years of age and William, aged 16, both of whom travelled back to England with the body for interment.[8] After the service, the remains were conveyed to the MGWR railway depot where they left Athlone on the evening mail train bound for interment in London.[9] Lambert was subsequently buried at Brookwood military cemetery. In early September 1921, the *Pall Mall Gazette* published details of Lambert's will and noted that he had left a legacy of £70,155 19s. 5d.[10] The following month, at a sitting of the Moate quarter sessions, Judge Fleming awarded Mrs Lambert £9,000 compensation for the death of her husband. Mrs Lambert, who was not entitled to a pension from military authorities due to her husband's legacy, was awarded £4,500 in her own name and £1,500 for each of her three children, her two older sons and her fifteen-month-old daughter, Rachel, who, the court stated, were 'poorer by the loss of their father to guide and direct them'.[11]

While details of Lambert's murder, court of inquiry proceedings and funeral were all documented extensively in the national press, the local newspapers remained tight-lipped about their interpretation of events when they were published the following Saturday. Perhaps, much like commercial interests in the town, the local newspapers were also wary of the repercussions if they engaged with Lambert's murder in a critical way. The local press, with the exception of the *Westmeath Examiner*, did not comment to any great extent on Lambert's murder. In its reporting of the event, the *Westmeath Examiner* simply reprinted a report from the *Freeman's Journal*, and in so doing avoided the dubious task of having to comment in its own name.[12] Despite these local tensions, news of Lambert's murder also reached the English press and a former comrade wrote to the *Yorkshire*

Post lamenting Lambert's passing:

> Your brief announcement of the death of Colonel Commandant
> T.S. Lambert has brought thousands of Yorkshiremen a sense
> of personal loss ... Soldiering was not merely his profession,
> but his hobby. He was deeply read in military history and was
> a sound tactician ... He was approachable and always ready to
> help and advise his officers.[13]

In the immediate aftermath of Lambert's death, Lieutenant Colonel
E.L. Challoner, Lambert's co-passenger on the evening of the murder,
became the commanding officer of the 13th Infantry Regiment. On
29 June, a week after the attack at Benown, Challoner issued a public
notice under regulations 9AA and 10 of the ROIR act and stipulated
that 'all cycles except motorcycles for which a permit has been
issued' were prohibited from travelling in an area bounded by the
River Inny on the north-eastern side of Lough Ree to Ballymahon
town and along the main road via Moyvore in a south-westerly
directly back towards Athlone. This cordon specifically encompassed
the area in which Lambert had been assassinated. The order also
included the stipulation that the Three Jolly Pigeons premises in
Glasson was required to cease trading at 6p.m. daily and warned that
a continuation and escalation of the outrages would result in more
'severe restrictions being imposed'.[14] The order was intended to be
operational from 10 July 1921 at 5a.m., just one day before the truce
came in to effect.

The attack at Benown and the subsequent demise of General
Lambert marked the most hostile period of the War of Independence
in the south Roscommon/Westmeath region. The murder of a British
officer in this manner was a significant coup for the IRA in the area,
whether that was the original intention or not, and it was only a
matter of time before retaliatory actions commenced. Clearly, the
burning of Knockcroghery was the first of these retributive attacks
(possibly due to the initial belief that those responsible for the ambush
came from that village), but once it emerged that the actual assailants
were from the eastern shore of the lake, reprisals in the Coosan area
were also instigated (fig. 1).

THE REPRISAL

On the same day as General Lambert's funeral took place, King George V was in Belfast for the opening of the Northern Irish parliament. In his speech to both houses, the king made a significant intervention in the War of Independence when he called for peace and reconciliation, stating:

> I speak from a full heart when I pray that my coming to Ireland today may prove to be the first step towards an end of strife amongst her people, whatever their race or creed. In that hope, I appeal to all Irishmen to pause, to stretch out the hand of forbearance and conciliation, to forgive and to forget, and to join in making for the land which they love a new era of peace, contentment, and goodwill.[15]

By late June 1921 both sides were open to the possibility of a truce. The IRA were experiencing an ongoing depletion of resources, in terms of both men and armaments. The British, by contrast, had significant resources, but did not have the topographical and local knowledge required to defeat the flying columns and their guerrilla tactics. Moreover, the cost of the war was increasingly difficult to justify politically. Another deciding factor was that the public in both Ireland and the United Kingdom seemed to want an end to the war. In an editorial in the *Freeman's Journal* the day after the king's speech in Belfast, the author noted that the speech was one that 'invites hope among those who are longing for an honourable Irish peace'. Despite this, there was also a visible anger in the editorial, which argued that the forbearance and conciliation that the king called for 'cannot be one-sided. The Knockcrogheries must cease', the paper continued.[16] For the time being at least, however, the Knockcroghery saga was far from over.

In their BMH witness statements, a number of volunteers from the greater Athlone area provided evidence about Lambert's death and their memory of the events that unfolded thereafter. In particular, four witnesses gave an almost uniform recollection of the reprisals that took place in the days after the military enquiry into Lambert's murder had concluded.[17] None of these witnesses linked the burning of Knockcroghery and the murder of Lambert, instead claiming that the reprisal for Lambert's murder was the sacking of a number of houses in the Coosan area a few days after his death.

Thomas Costello recalled that military activity in the area increased after the murder and searches of the countryside as well as on the islands in Lough Ree between Coosan and the western shore took place. The brigade HQ was situated in the area at the time but 'escaped detection' in these searches.[18] He continued: 'The military did not carry out any reprisals, but after a few days, the Tans came into the area and burned the houses of seven families'.[19] Henry O'Brien concurred with this and added: 'They acted very callously in doing so, not even allowing the inhabitants to get dressed when they took them out of their beds, or to collect any of their belongings'.[20]

O'Brien was the captain of Coosan company and claimed that there were about eighty men in the company, making it the largest in the brigade. This alone meant that the attention of the authorities would have been drawn to the area. There is little doubt, however, that antagonisms between the local communities in Coosan and Glasson and the authorities in the area had been strained even before Lambert's murder. The previous weekend a number of people who had been having a picnic on the shores of the lake at Coosan were 'rounded up and questioned' by 'crown forces in large numbers fully equipped'. The young men were searched, with some brought for questioning to the military barracks afterwards. This, apparently, was in relation to 'four soldiers who had been held up' by armed men the week before.[21] A few days after the murder of Lambert, the *Freeman's Journal*, perhaps concurring with the evidence given by Costello and O'Brien to the BMH, recorded that

> Fearing reprisals after the shooting of Colonel Commandant Lambert ... the residents of Glasson village removed the greater part of their furniture. Some of them went to neighbouring houses and others spent the night on the roadside. Nothing untoward happened and most of them returned home yesterday.[22]

Within days, however, seven families had had their homes destroyed.

Despite the negotiations that were taking place in officialdom regarding a potential truce in the war, the situation in south

Roscommon and Westmeath continued to worsen. In retaliation for the burning of the seven houses in Coosan, Thomas Costello recalled that 'an order was received from GHQ that we were to burn an equal number of houses belonging to supporters of the British regime as a counter reprisal'.[23] It was decided that although there were a number of potential smaller loyalist targets in the area, a more effective approach would be an attack on Moydrum Castle (fig. 1), the country seat of Lord Castlemaine, the king's lieutenant for Co. Westmeath. Significantly, Castlemaine had no involvement in politics and had not been involved in the war up to this point.[24] The eighteenth-century mansion, which had been in the family for over a century, however, represented a very appealing prospect for the local IRA. Michael McCormack, adjunct to the Drumraney Battalion, noted that the burning of Moydrum Castle 'put a curb on the British Forces resorting to reprisals in the future'.[25] It is also significant to note that as the War of Independence came to an end, high-profile marks such as large country houses that were, in many ways, the personification of British presence in Ireland, were seen as valuable targets for the IRA. They held a place of distinction in Irish society, and their demise at the hands of the IRA was symbolic as well as destructive.[26] In the final report on the war in Ireland compiled by the War Office, it was noted that in the last weeks of the war, specifically from June 1921 until the truce on 11 July, '27 cases of the burning of houses by the IRA in the 5th Division area were reported. Portumna Castle, Co. Galway, and Moydrum Castle in Co. Westmeath were the largest of these houses'.[27]

Costello was the commanding officer of the Athlone flying column on the night that Moydrum Castle was burned. In his BMH witness statement, Costello did concede that there were smaller houses owned by Protestants in the area but concluded that 'it would not be fair to burn those people's houses for something which was not their fault'.[28] By extension, it is difficult to comprehend how this logic did not extend to Lady Castlemaine in Moydrum Castle and perhaps it does suggest that Irish country houses were a new strategic departure for the IRA as the war drew to a close.[29]

On the night of the burning, 3 July 1921, just over a week before the truce came into effect, Lady Castlemaine and her daughter, Ms Handcook, were in residence in the castle. Costello stated that he mobilized 'about 20 men' but, in the aftermath of the burning, the press noted this number to be closer to forty.[30] Having been refused access to the castle, the attackers used hammers to gain entry, after which they met the butler and Lady Castlemaine and demanded keys to the stores. Costello informed Lady Castlemaine of their intent and she requested some time to gather some personal belongings. Although Costello pointed out that no such time had been afforded to the families in Coosan and Mount Temple, or indeed Knockcroghery for that matter, he allowed Lady Castlemaine an extended period of time to collect her possessions. Costello recalled:

> I gave her the time she required and also ten men to help her with the task and they took out about ten boxes of materials … Two armchairs were taken out of the castle and put down for the Lady and her daughter to sit on … I informed Lady Castlemaine that we were not criminals and were acting on the orders of GHQ of the IRA and that the burning of her home was a reprisal for the burning done by England's Black and Tans. She was very dignified under the circumstances and never winced. She thanked me for my cooperation in saving her treasures and assured me that she quite understood.[31]

In the compensation hearing that followed in October, the court heard that the IRA used a combination of petrol and paraffin obtained from the stores on-site to start the fire.[32] Henry O'Brien, who was also present on the night of the burning, recalled in his witness statement to the BMH that: 'The place was liberally sprinkled with petrol and paraffin, holes being made in the floors and ceilings to give the flames ventilation'.[33] In a paradoxical divergence at the court hearing, it was noted how Costello had 'expressed his sorrow that he had to burn the house' and the fact that he allowed Lady Castlemaine an extended period of time and apportioned her some of his men to help with the task of collecting her valuables might suggest that Costello was not entirely convinced of the merits of destroying the castle.[34] Despite this, at 4a.m. on 3 July 1921, the castle was set on fire and as Costello concluded: 'having assured ourselves that it would be totally destroyed, we saluted Lady Castlemaine and withdrew'.[35]

At the compensation hearing, Lord Castlemaine stated that he wished to rebuild the property and had no desire to live anywhere else. Accordingly, the claim he lodged was for £200,000 for the damage to his property. Mr Hicks, the engineer, however, stated that it would cost £84,759 to rebuild the castle. Judge Fleming subsequently awarded Castlemaine £101,359 for the attack on his residence at Moydrum and for the loss of furniture and personal belongings. After Castlemaine's case was heard and assessed by the Shaw/Wood-Renton commission, however, this amount was reduced to £66,174.[36] In a further bizarre development in the Moydrum affair, Castlemaine took two of his former employees, Michael Grady and Patrick Delaney, to court in August 1921 on charges of larceny which occurred on the night of the fire. Grady and Delaney were charged with stealing a fur coat, two dress shirts, a smoking jacket, a suitcase and a bicycle. They were subsequently sentenced to six and four months hard labour respectively.[37]

The enactment of the truce on 11 July signalled the end of the War of Independence in south Roscommon and Westmeath. The last three weeks of the war were undoubtedly the most antagonistic of the period and the ostensibly unintended murder of General Lambert set in train a series of events that disrupted hundreds of lives in the region irrespective of race, creed or social class. With the benefit of hindsight, it can be argued that the people of Knockcroghery were collateral damage in a case of mistaken identity and their unsolicited inclusion in this narrative, coupled with their apparent exclusion from the official record of it, unjustifiably depreciates the impact of the war on the village. Despite this, in the days and weeks after the burning, the people of Knockcroghery came together with a resilience that was focused on reconstruction of their village.

THE RECONSTRUCTION

While attacks and reprisals on the eastern shore of Lough Ree continued to escalate during the final weeks of the War of Independence, the people of Knockcroghery were faced with the task of trying to rebuild both their lives and their village. In the days after the burning, a local committee of the White Cross was established, the composition of which was reflective of the cooperative, non-denominational and apolitical character of the parent organization. Jimmy Murray recalled that 'At that time there was an organization called the Green (*sic*) Cross … an organization that had funds that were distributed to people they thought were in a bad way after the burning'.[38] In a subsequent interview, he noted that 'My father [John S. Murray] … was on the committee with Canon Kelly and Mr Humphries and two of the shopkeepers'.[39] Once the committee was established and had been allocated funding, they 'distributed clothes and money to those who needed it at the time'.[40]

The White Cross was a charitable organization with close links to the Society of Friends. It was established in February 1921 after James Green Douglas, a Quaker, Irish nationalist and future Senator in the Irish Free State, had received a cheque for $25,000 from the American Committee for Relief in Ireland. The American committee, which had close links to, but remained separate from, the Society of Friends, requested that the donation would not be used for political purposes. A second donation of $25,000 was made shortly after the first and Douglas promptly set about the task of forming a committee. On 2 February 1921 the *Evening Echo* reported that

> At a meeting in Dublin yesterday … the Lord Mayor [of Dublin, Laurence O'Neill] … stated the object of the meeting was to form an Irish White Cross Society for the relief of distress caused through the present campaign in Ireland. He announced the receipt of 50,000 dollars … for the purposes of relief and reconstruction.[41]

A committee was then formally established with Cardinal Logue being appointed as the president of the Irish White Cross. Members of Sinn Féin, however, specifically Michael Collins and Arthur Griffith, as well as unionists such as Prof. Edward Culverwell of Trinity College and a former British army captain, David Robertson, were also appointed, the latter as acting secretary to the standing executive committee. Douglas himself was also heavily involved in the organization.[42]

It is quite fitting that it was to the Irish White Cross that the people of Knockcroghery turned in search of relief. At its core, the organization was characterized by unity and sought to reject sectarian divisions within communities, something that both Canon Kelly and Revd Humphries had been advocating long before the burning of the village took place. Within the first seven months of its establishment, the Irish White Cross had raised and distributed £1,374,795 of aid to communities across Ireland in need of relief.[43] Philanthropic donations were received from North America, England, Scotland and other non-specified countries. The organization also received a donation of £5,149 from Pope Benedict XV. A number of sub-committees were established including a fund for the relief of disabled persons, an orphaned children's fund and a reconstruction commission.[44]

According to the *Report of the Irish White Cross*, a total of £7,222 10s. was awarded to the people of Co. Roscommon, from its inception up to 31 August 1922, as part of the 'personal relief' fund. Of this, £716 was allocated to the people of Knockcroghery.[45] By comparison, £14 and £85 were the amounts that were awarded to Tubberclare and Glasson communities respectively, as part of the personal relief fund. This highlights the level of complete destruction and destitution experienced by the people of Knockcroghery in the aftermath of the burning.[46] A further £9,075 was allocated to Co. Roscommon through the funds distributed by the reconstruction commission.[47] What exact proportion of this was distributed to Knockcroghery is unknown, but given the level of damage, a portion of this figure would likely have been allocated to reconstructing the village.

There is little doubt that in the days and weeks after the burning of the village, the initiative and fortitude exhibited by the village's spiritual leaders and business people, and indeed by the population more generally, resulted in the community emerging from the burning with a determination to reconstruct the village and regain their lives. Before this could be fully achieved, however, the complex question of compensation needed to be addressed.

A total of nineteen compensation claims were lodged with Roscommon Circuit Court in the aftermath of the burning.[48] These claims were handled by three solicitors, Mr Neilan, Mr Hannon and Mr McSherry, and were heard and decreed on by Judge Wakely on 25 October 1921. The charges were levied on the county and its ratepayers, meaning that those who owned property were responsible for meeting the decrees as awarded by the circuit court judge. The claims ranged from £100 to £22,000 and amounted to just under £100,000 in total. Only about 33 per cent of the total claim was actually decreed. Judge Wakely awarded a combined total of £32,230 to the claimants from Knockcroghery for malicious damages caused by the fires on the night of the attack.[49]

At the hearing it was stated that the burning was a 'reprisal for the shooting of General Lambert on the Westmeath side of Athlone' on 20 June.[50] DI Cole of the RIC put on the public record that, 'although he made every possible enquiry, he was unable to trace the perpetrators', and continued that 'it was not customary for lorries to be used by other than crown forces'.[51] Mr Hannon, one of the solicitors representing the claimants, then stated before the court that there were witnesses 'to prove that the perpetrators came in military lorries, but they could not be got to give evidence'.[52] A summary of the claims lodged and decrees awarded are outlined in Table 1.[53] The highest amount of compensation was awarded to Bridget Curley for malicious damage to her dwelling house, pipe factory, plant and machinery. She was awarded £6,190 plus costs and witness expenses. Her original claim had been lodged for £20,000. Similarly, Andrew and Patrick Curley claimed £15,000 for malicious damage to their house, factory and machinery and were awarded £5,994. Aside from pipe makers, the Jackson sisters, Annie and Dinah, filed £22,000 for malicious damage to a dwelling house, licensed premises, stock in trade and furniture. Judge Wakely awarded them £6,140, but the Jackson sisters fell victim to the Shaw Commission and this award was later reduced. Fr Kelly made two separate claims, each for £1,000. The first referred to the loss of a motor car and personal injuries and the second was related to personal effects. He was awarded £275 and a further £50 for consequential damages. The *Roscommon Herald* noted that these referred to 'injury to the presbytery and the destruction of book-cases and valuable books'.[54] William Roper was the main landlord in the village and he owned eight of the houses that were burned in the attack. Roper, who was anxious to sell his interests, lodged a claim of £7,000 and Judge Wakely awarded £3,121 in compensation and, according to the *Roscommon Herald*, the judge 'arranged that for this purpose [selling the properties] 21 years purchase to be deduced from the decrees'.[55]

Nonetheless, what was awarded and what was likely to be paid to the claimants were two very different things. As FitzPatrick noted, 'most malicious injury claims were presented with the aim of publicizing atrocities rather than actually securing compensation'

Table 1: Summary of compensation claims and decrees awarded by Roscommon Circuit Court in the matter of the burning of Knockcroghery, 21 June 1921

Name	Amount sought	Amount awarded by Roscommon Circuit Court	Amended amount awarded by Shaw Commission	Reason
Misses A. & D. Jackson	£22,000	£6,140 + costs	£3,750 + costs	Maliciously destroying by fire dwelling house, licensed premises, stock-in-trade, furniture
Mrs Bridget Curley	£20,000	£6,190 + costs	£4,700 + costs	Maliciously destroying by fire dwelling house and furniture
Andrew and Patrick Curley	£15,000	£5,994 + costs	£3,125 + costs	Maliciously destroying dwelling house, pipe factory and machinery
Denis O'Brien	£12,000	£5,627 + costs	£3,217 + costs	Maliciously destroying by fire dwelling house, licensed premises, drapery premises, and contents
Mrs Mary Anne Lyons	£6,000	£2,018 + costs	£1,400 + costs	Maliciously destroying by fire dwelling house, stable and furniture
Patrick FitzGerald	£5,000	£1,221 + costs	£750 + costs	Maliciously destroying by fire dwelling house, stable and furniture
Catherine Cunnane	£5,000	£1,914 + costs	n/avl	Maliciously destroying 2 dwelling houses & furniture
Edward Gordan	£5,000	£1,014 + costs	£560 + costs	Maliciously destroying dwelling houses & furniture
Bernard FitzGerald	£1,000	£752 + costs	£440 + costs	Maliciously destroying by fire dwelling house and furniture
Revd B. Kelly	£1,000	£307 + costs	£250 + costs	Maliciously partially destroying dwelling house, furniture and library
Misses B. & E. Cunnane	£500	£86 + costs	£80 + costs	Maliciously destroying by fire clothing and effects
Patrick Kelleher	£500	£360 + costs	£100 + costs	Maliciously destroying by fire furniture and clothing
Bernard Curley	£300	£74 + costs	£57 + costs	Maliciously destroying by fire bicycle, clothing and books
William Murtagh	£300	£290 + costs	£95 + costs	Maliciously destroying by fire furniture and clothing
Kate Nealon	£150	£32 + costs	£28 + costs	Maliciously burning a quantity of clothing
Frederick Jackson	£150	£100 + costs	£67 + costs	Maliciously destroying clothing and personal effects
Mrs Meta Anderson	£100	£55 + costs	£40 + costs	Maliciously destroying clothing and personal effects
Annie Geraghty	£100	£35 + costs	£40 + costs	Maliciously destroying clothing and personal effects
Daniel Dempsey	£100	£21 + costs	£15 + costs	Maliciously destroying clothing and personal effects
* Michael Coyle, Carnagh	£1,000	£5	n/avl	Shooting of father

* Michael Coyle was the son of Patrick Coyle, the blacksmith shot by an RIC patrol on 1 June 1921 while he was attending a sick horse at Hubert Murphy's house.

because the ratepayers in each county were not able to afford the escalating personal injuries bill that was being levied on them as a result of the war.[56]

After the incarnation of the Irish Free State, there were a number of legacy issues that needed to be addressed between the British government and its Irish counterpart. One of these issues was the question of compensation. In May 1922 a Compensation Commission was established under the chairmanship of Lord Shaw of Dunfermline. Shaw was a Scottish liberal who was well suited to the task. The purpose of the commission was to investigate each of the 37,000 claims that had been lodged. Frustrated at the slow rate of progress, Shaw resigned his chairmanship in November 1922 and was replaced, eventually, by Sir Alexander Wood-Renton who had some previous experience in the area. Importantly, from a local perspective at least, the introduction of the commission relieved the ratepayers in each county of the responsibility of having to pay the awards and now the onus fell to the ministry of finance to pay the compensation. Each government agreed to pay the injury claims perpetrated by its own supporters. Essentially, this meant that in the case of Knockcroghery, which, it was agreed, was an act of reprisal, the compensation was to be paid by the British treasury.

The first of the Knockcroghery claims was heard by the Shaw Commission in March 1923, at which time the compensation awarded to the Jackson sisters was almost halved, from £6,140 to £3,750. The same fate befell Denis O'Brien, another publican in the village, who had his compensation significantly reduced from just under £6,000 to £3,217.[57] Other claimants from the village, in particular the two families of Curleys that were involved in pipe production, also had their compensation reduced. Despite the reductions, the families were arguably in a better position by having their claims processed as part of the Shaw Commission as there was more chance of receiving money from the British treasury than from either the county ratepayers or the ministry of finance in Dublin.

After the compensation was awarded by the commission, it appears that payment was imminent. Annie Jackson's claim was heard by the commission in early March and within three months, almost exactly two years after the fire, the *Roscommon Journal* published a notice seeking tenders for the reconstruction of Jackson's 'shop and residence at Knockcroghery'.[58] The plans, which had been drawn by architect M.J. Leech of Ballymoe, could be viewed at Jackson's premises in Knockcroghery. After the tendering process, a local builder named Foley from Ballymurray was awarded the contract and work began.

As General Lambert and his travelling companions left Killinure House on that evening in June 1921, few could have predicted the extent of the consequences of his murder. Within the space of three weeks, Lambert had been murdered, Knockcroghery had been burned, a dying craft had been wiped out, seven families in Coosan and Mount Temple had lost their homes and Moydrum Castle had been destroyed (fig. 1). All of this happened within the context of police and military investigations, a court of inquiry, a high-profile funeral, an impassioned monarchical speech and complex truce negotiations.

Conclusion

One glaring question remains: why was there no reprisal by the IRA for the burning of the village of Knockcroghery? In wartime, the destruction of an entire village by an adversary, whether as a result of misinformation or not, surely warrants some type of retributive action? Yet, there was none. A few days later, when seven houses were burned in Coosan and Mount Temple in reprisal for Lambert's killing, Costello recorded those orders sent from GHQ to target an equal number of loyalist homes in that area.[1] Why was no similar instruction sent from GHQ to the 4th South Roscommon Brigade or indeed Pat Madden's flying column?

There are some factors that might explain the absence of a reprisal for Knockcroghery. First, the village was burned the day before King George V's speech in Belfast where he called for reconciliation and peace. Perhaps this intervention and the prospect of a truce impacted any potential plans for a reprisal. Second, there was likely a paucity of arms in the area, which would have frustrated the effectiveness of any potential retaliation.[2] Third, it is possible that there was a lack of strong leadership in south Roscommon at this stage of the war. This had also been apparent in the murder of RIC constable William Potter the previous year, and is further evidenced by the nature of the warfare in south Roscommon during this period, which was repeatedly characterized by smaller actions, such as cutting telegraph wires or raiding mail trains. The crown forces' reprisals for these acts came usually in the form of house searches and arrests. Across Lough Ree, as has been shown here, the nature of IRA activity and the reprisals that could be expected were of a more egregious nature, perhaps explained by the larger numbers engaged in IRA activity and more effective leadership on the eastern side of the lake. Fourthly, even though there was a big house of importance in the parish, namely Lord Crofton's demesne at Mote Park, there appeared to be an inclination towards tolerance and cooperation in the area. This is not to suggest that some type of idyllic utopia existed, but rather a mutual respect within the community, as evidenced by the response of Revd Humphries and his wife in the aftermath of the burning itself. However, are these reasons compelling enough to explain the lack of a retaliation for burning an entire village, which resulted in the destruction of the local economy and at least fifteen homeless families?

While each of these reasons, or indeed a combination of them, is plausible, there is also a troubling alternative explanation. As part of her research on the Irish Volunteers in Roscommon, Kathleen Hegarty-Thorne briefly examined the burning of Knockcroghery and suggested that the burning may have had little to do with Lambert's death and more to do with the intended use of the abducted Hotchkiss gun commandeered by the IRA in the Scramogue ambush the previous March.[3] Hegarty-Thorne suggests that Pat Madden, the O/C of the 3rd South Roscommon Brigade, intended to place the gun on the outskirts of the village, on the Athlone side near the railway station, and use it to ambush the military as they travelled between Athlone and Roscommon in tenders.[4] Hegarty-Thorne notes that on a particular day, the wood that was regularly brought to Knockcroghery for onward distribution by rail was not stored in its usual location, but rather stacked strategically and defensively around the village. An informant, she claims, told crown forces about the planned attack and they were so enraged by the abrasive nature of the proposed ambush that they arrived in the village and burned it. Despite the problematic timeline – for instance, why would the crown forces arrive in Knockcroghery at 1a.m. if this was the case? – there may be some truth to this version of events. Patrick Lennon in his BMH witness statement recalled an IRA informant named Heary being shot outside Knockcroghery and Lennon associates the death of this informant with the burning of the village.[5] Not only is there not any evidence, however, aside from this brief testimony, to suggest Pat Madden and his flying column did intend to attack crown forces with the Hotchkiss gun in Knockcroghery, but it is also plausible that it was Heary who told the crown forces that Lambert's murderers had escaped to the western shores of Lough Ree and this is why the village was targeted.

Ultimately, a historian can only follow the evidence, and in this instance the evidence overwhelmingly suggests that the burning of

Knockcroghery was a misinformed, impulsive, retributive action to avenge the murder of Colonel-Commandant Thomas Stanton Lambert. It was a spontaneous, emotional response, most likely by men from the 1st Leicestershire Regiment, rather than the Black and Tans per se, who, seeking revenge for their fallen comrade, acted on false intelligence that resulted in the burning of the village. The misinformation in turn resulted in the demise of an already dying craft, the decimation of the local economy, the emergence of fifteen homeless families and the subsequent accelerated emigration of the village's young people. It also led to the development of strong communal bonds, however, and a collective memory that promoted a shared communal identity that inevitably changed the course of the village for the next one hundred years.

Notes

ABBREVIATIONS

ADRIC	Auxiliary Division of the Royal Irish Constabulary
BMH	Bureau of Military History
DED	district electoral division
DI	detective inspector
EE	*Evening Echo*
FJ	*Freeman's Journal*
GAA	Gaelic Athletic Association
GHQ	general headquarters
GOC	general officer commanding
HQ	headquarters
II	*Irish Independent*
IRA	Irish Republican Army
MA	Military Archives
MGWR	Midland Great Western Railway
MSPC	Military Service Pension Collection
NAI	National Archives of Ireland
O/C	officer commanding
POW	prisoner of war
RAMC	Royal Army Medical Corps
RASC	Royal Army Service Corps
RE	Royal Engineers
RH	*Roscommon Herald*
RIC	Royal Irish constabulary
RJ	*Roscommon Journal*
RJWR	*Roscommon Journal and Western Reporter*
ROIR	Regulation of Order in Ireland Regulations
UCD	University College Dublin
WE	*Westmeath Examiner*
WI	*Westmeath Independent*
WS	witness statement(s)

INTRODUCTION

1 Victoria Barracks was renamed Custume Barracks in 1922.

2 Jacinta Prunty, *Maps and map-making in local history* (Dublin, 2004); John Cunningham, *Conquest and land in Ireland: the transplantation to Connacht, 1649–1680* (Woodbridge, 2011); Thomas Larcom, *The history of the survey of Ireland commonly called the Down Survey* (Dublin, 1851).

3 Sir Charles Coote is mentioned in the deposition of Sir Lucas Dillon, a prominent landowner in the greater environs of Knockcroghery, as well as in the depositions of Michael Boyer and Hugh O Mannin. Coote's army was largely responsible for opening up Connacht to Cromwellian forces after taking the town of Athlone in June 1651. For more, see 1641 Depositions available at Trinity College Dublin, https://1641. tcd.ie, last accessed 23 Sept. 2020.

4 Charles Townshend, 'The Irish Republican Army and the development of guerrilla warfare, 1916–21', *English Historical Review*, 94 (1979), pp 318–45;

Joost Augusteijn, *From public defiance to guerrilla warfare: the experience of ordinary volunteers in the Irish War of Independence* (Dublin, 1996); David FitzPatrick, 'The geography of Irish nationalism, 1910–1921', *Past & Present*, 78 (1978), pp 113–44.

5   Marie Coleman, *County Longford and the Irish revolution, 1910–1923* (Dublin, 2003); John Burke, *Roscommon: the Irish Revolution, 1912–1923* (Dublin, 2021) and John Burke, *Athlone, 1900–1923: politics, revolution and civil war* (Dublin, 2015).

6   Summary of police reports, 22–30 June 1921 (National Archives, Kew, CO904/146).

7   William Gacquin, 'Knockcroghery: clay and pipes in Knockcroghery', *Rindoon Journal*, 4 (2017), pp 131–49 and Extract from Benjamin Greene's diaries, transcribed by Mai Byrne, 'The diaries of Benjamin Greene of Hill House, Lecarrow – Part 1', *Rindoon Journal*, 1 (2004), pp 135–50.

8   Interview with Jimmy Murray by Declan Coyne, *Roscommon Champion 75th anniversary magazine* (Roscommon, 2003), pp 88–9.

9   Project Knockcroghery, *The burning of Knockcroghery, 1921*, available at www. youtube.com/watch?v=UnKf7NRJZgg, last accessed 25 Sept. 2021.

I. THE VILLAGE

1   Isaac Weld, *Statistical survey of the county of Roscommon* (Dublin, 1832), p. 508.

2   Ibid., p. 509.

3   Ibid.

4   Samuel Lewis, *A topographical dictionary of Ireland, comprising the several counties, cities, boroughs etc.*, ii (London, 1837), p. 239.

5   William Gacquin, 'A household account from County Roscommon, 1733–4' in Denis Cronin, Jim Galligan and Karina Holton (eds), *Irish fairs and markets: studies in local history* (Dublin, 2001), pp 99–124 at p. 112.

6   Lewis, *Topographical dictionary*, p. 239; George S. Measom, *The official illustrated guide to the Midland Great Western and Dublin and Drogheda Railways …* (London, 1867), p. 325. See also Gacquin, 'A household account', p. 104.

7   Measom, *Guide to the Midland Great Western and Dublin and Drogheda Railways*, p. 325.

8   1901 Census of Ireland, returns for Knockcroghery, DED [92], available at: NAI, www.census.nationalarchives.ie, last accessed 1 Oct. 2020.

9   The records indicate that some census pages are missing. 1901 Census of Ireland, Returns for Knockcroghery; 1911 Census of Ireland, returns for Knockcroghery town, DED [92], available at www.census.nationalarchives. ie, last accessed 1 Oct. 2020; 1926 Census of Saorstat Eireann, abstract, table 11 – population, area and valuation by district electoral division, available at www.cso.ie/en/media/csoie/census/census1926results/volume1/C_1926_V1_T11.pdf, last accessed 1 Oct. 2020, p. 72.

10 *Report and tables showing the number, ages, conjugal condition and destinations of the emigrants from each county and province in Ireland during the year 1919, also the occupations of the emigrants and the number of emigrants who left each port, 1–10* [C 1414], HC 1921, xli, 401.

11 *WI*, 2 Aug. 1919.

12 Extract from Benjamin Greene's diary, 16 June 1920, pt 1, p. 144.

13 Ibid., p. 145.

14 Lewis, *Topographical dictionary*, p. 239; Weld, *Statistical survey*, p. 509.

15 Weld, *Statistical survey*, p. 510.

16 *RJ*, 25 Nov. 1921.

17 Reg Jackson, Philomena Jackson and Roger Price, *Ireland and the Bristol clay-pipe trade* (Bristol, 1983), p. 38.

18 Schools Folklore Commission available at www.duchas.ie/ec/cbes, last accessed 26 Sept. 2020.

19 Seán Ó Súilleabháin, *Irish wake amusements* (Cork, 1967), p. 1; see also Anne Ridge, *Death customs in rural Ireland: traditional funerary rites in the Irish midlands* (Syracuse, NY, 2009), p. 66.

20 Weld, *Statistical survey*, p. 510.

21 Census record for Thomas Buckley, fo. 140, Parish of Killinvoy, Census of Elphin, 1749 available at www. findmypast.ie, last accessed 25 Sept. 2020. See also Colin Rynne, *Industrial Ireland, 1750–1930: an archaeology* (Cork, 2006), pp 180–1; Gacquin, 'A household account', p. 112.

22 Weld, *Statistical survey*, p. 510.

23 Ibid.

24 Ibid., p. 513.
25 Mary Mulvihill, *Ingenious Ireland: a county-by-county exploration of Irish mysteries and marvels* (Dublin, 2019), p. 252.
26 *RJ*, 25 Nov. 1921.
27 *RH*, 5 Nov. 1921. The remark was articulated at the compensation hearing for PJ Curley in late Oct. 1921.
28 1901 Census of Ireland, returns for Knockcroghery, DED [92], available at www.census.nationalarchives.ie, last accessed 1 Oct. 2020, 1911 Census of Ireland, returns for Knockcroghery town, DED [92], available at www. census.nationalarchives.ie, last accessed 1 Oct. 2020.
29 1901 Census of Ireland, returns for Knockcroghery.
30 Ibid.
31 1911 Census of Ireland, returns for Knockcroghery town.
32 The enumerations in this analysis differ from the enumerations calculated by William Gacquin in his article on Knockcroghery clay pipes as different methodologies were used by each author: see Gacquin, 'Knockcroghery', pp 140–1.
33 Mulvihill, *Ingenious Ireland*, p. 252.
34 Ibid.
35 *WI*, 22 May 1920.
36 Extract from Benjamin Greene's diary, 14 Jan. 1920, Byrne, 'The diaries', pt 1, p. 137.
37 Extract from Benjamin Greene's diary, 2 Jan. 1920, Byrne, 'The diaries', pt 1, p. 136.
38 Extract from Benjamin Greene's diary, 16 Sept. 1920, Byrne, 'The diaries', pt 1, p. 146.
39 Extract from Benjamin Greene's diary, 6 Jan. 1920, Byrne, 'The diaries', pt 1, p. 140.
40 *WI*, 10 July 1920.
41 *RJWR*, 26 Feb. 1916.
42 Ibid., 8 July 1914.
43 Extract from Benjamin Greene's diary, 3 July 1920, Byrne, 'The diaries', pt 1, p. 144.

2. THE WAR
1 *FJ*, 20 June 1916.
2 *RJWR*, 15 Dec. 1918.
3 Brigade Activity Report, 4th Battalion, South Roscommon Brigade

(Military Archives, Dublin, MA/MSPC/A/27), ii, p. 16, available at www. militaryarchives.ie/collections/online-collections/military-service-pensions-collection-1916–1923/brigade-activities, last accessed 15 Nov. 2020.
4 Ibid.
5 Ibid.
6 Brigade Activity Report, 4th Battalion, South Roscommon Brigade, p. 30.
7 Lecarrow barracks had been closed the previous week: extract from Benjamin Greene's diary, 6 Jan. 1920, Byrne, 'The diaries', pt 1, p. 141.
8 Kathleen Hegarty-Thorne, *They put the flag a flyin': the Roscommon volunteers, 1916–1923* (Eugene, OR, 2005), pp 91–114.
9 *Offaly Independent*, 28 Feb. 1920.
10 Ibid.
11 Brigade Activity Report, 4th Battalion, South Roscommon Brigade, p. 30.
12 Extract from Benjamin Greene's diary, 21 May 1920 and 26 Nov. 1920, Byrne, 'The diaries', pt 1, pp 143, 149.
13 *WI*, 28 Aug. 1920. See also Eunan O'Halpin and Daithí Ó Corráin, *The dead of the Irish Revolution* (New Haven, CT, 2020), p. 165.
14 *WI*, 28 Aug. 1920.
15 Ibid. See also Brigade Activity Report, 4th Battalion, South Roscommon Brigade, p. 22.
16 Extract from Benjamin Greene's diary, 27 Aug. 1920, Byrne, 'The diaries', pt 1, p. 146.
17 *WI*, 28 Aug. 1920. See also Richard Abbot, *Police casualties in Ireland* (Cork, 2019), p. 146.
18 Matthew Davis, BMH, WS691, p. 7, available at www.militaryarchives.ie/collections/online-collections/bureau-of-military-history-1913–1921, last accessed 1 Oct. 2021. All references to the BMH witness statements hereafter can be found at the above URL.
19 Thomas Kelly, BMH, WS701, p. 8.
20 Ibid.
21 *II*, 31 Aug. 1920.
22 *WI*, 11 Sept. 1920.
23 War Office, *Record of the rebellion in Ireland, 1920–21, and the part played by the army in dealing with it*, i (London, 1923), p. 18. For extended discussion on the Black and Tans and Auxiliary forces in

Ireland, see D.M. Lesson, *The Black and Tans: British police and auxiliaries in the Irish War of Independence* (Oxford, 2011); W.H. Kautt, *Ambushes and armour: the Irish rebellion, 1919–1921* (Dublin, 2010).

24 War Office, *Record of the rebellion in Ireland, 1920–21, and the part played by the army in dealing with it*, iv, appendix XX (London, 1923), p. 117.

25 *WI*, 23 Oct. 1920.

26 John Burke, *Athlone, 1900–23*, e-copy, ch. 6.

27 Ibid.

28 Ibid.

29 Ibid.

30 War Office, *Record of the rebellion in Ireland*, iv, pp 99–100.

31 Brigade Activity Report, 1st Battalion, Athlone Brigade, Military Archives, Dublin, MA/MSPC/A/68, p. 26 available at www.militaryarchives.ie/collections/online-collections/military-service-pensions-collection-1916–1923/brigade-activities, last accessed 15 Nov. 2020.

32 War Office, *Record of the rebellion in Ireland*, iv, p. 99.

33 Hegarty-Thorne, *Flag a flyin'*, pp 181–6.

34 Burke, *Roscommon: the Irish Revolution*, p. 105.

35 Hegarty-Thorne, *Flag a flyin'*, p. 182.

36 For a more detailed exploration of the Clonfin ambush, see Paul O'Brien, *Havoc: the Auxiliaries in Ireland's War of Independence* (Cork, 2017), ch. 17; Marie Coleman, *County Longford and the Irish revolution, 1910–1923* (Dublin, 2003), pp 126–7; Kautt, *Ambushes and armour*, pp 167–70.

37 For extensive analysis on MacEoin, see Padraic O'Farrell, *The blacksmith of Ballinalee: the life of Sean McEoin* (Dublin and Cork, 1981).

38 Sean MacEoin, BMH, WS1716, pt ii, pp 148–55.

39 Ibid., p. 171.

40 Ibid., p. 174.

41 *FJ*, 15 June 1921.

42 Burke, *Roscommon: the Irish Revolution*, pp 108–10. See also Joseph McKenna, *Guerrilla warfare in the Irish War of Independence, 1919–1921* (Jefferson, NC, 2011), pp 246–50.

43 Frank Simons, BM, WS770, p. 24. For detailed descriptions of the Scramogue

ambush, see Martin Fallon, BMH, WS 1121, p. 13; Luke Duffy, BMH, WS 661, p. 18; Patrick Mullolly, BMH, WS 955, p. 19, available at www.militaryarchives.ie and Interview with Martin Fallon, UCD Archives, Ernie O'Malley Notebooks, p. 17b/131 and Interview with Frank Simons, UCD Archives, Ernie O'Malley Notebooks, p. 17b/137.

44 War Office, *Record of the rebellion in Ireland, 1920–21*, iv, p. 52.

45 Constable John Duffy, BMH, WS580, pp 21–2.

46 Ibid., p. 22.

47 Ibid., p. 23.

48 Thomas Kelly, BMH, WS701, p. 9. Hegarty-Thorne identifies a number of men from the Knockcroghery company that were involved in this activity: *Flag a flyin'*, pp 218–22.

49 Ibid.

50 *II*, 4 June 1921. Hubert Murphy and his two brothers, Thomas and William, were sought by the RIC for a number of outrages. Murphy was the O/C of St John's company.

51 *II*, 4 June 1921.

52 Hegarty-Thorne, *Flag a flyin'*, p. 101. See also Kevin Coyle, 'Coyles of the Forge', *Rindoon Journal*, 1 (2004), pp 23–7.

53 War Office, *Record of the rebellion in Ireland*, iv, pp 42–3.

54 Ibid., p. 43.

55 Ibid.

56 Ibid., i, p. 45.

57 Ibid.

58 War Office, *Record of the rebellion in Ireland*, iv, p. 105.

59 Local lore suggests that the aim was to capture Lambert and hold him hostage until MacEoin had been released.

60 Thomas Costello, BMH, WS1296, pp 21–2.

61 Brigade Activity Report, 'C' company, 2nd (Drumraney) Battalion, Athlone Brigade, Military Archives, Dublin, MA/MSPC/A/68/2, p. 36, available at www.militaryarchives.ie/collections/online-collections/military-service-pensions-collection-1916–1923/brigade-activities, last accessed 15 Nov. 2020. Furthermore, very little information about the ambush is recorded in the Ernie O'Malley Notebooks (UCDA/P17b/) available at UCD archives.

62 Brigade Activity Report, 'C' company, 2nd (Drumraney) Battalion, p. 36; *FJ*, 21 June 1921.

63 Daily summaries of reports on outrages, June–Aug. 1921 (National Archives, Kew, CO904/146).

3. THE BURNING

1 War Office, *Record of the rebellion in Ireland*, iv, p. 54.

2 *Irish Times*, 22 June 1921. In his BMH witness statement, Patrick Lennon from the Summerhill company of the Volunteers identifies an informant named Heary who he associates with the burning of the village: Patrick Lennon, BMH, WS1336, p. 13.

3 Summary of police reports, 22–30 June 1921 (National Archives, Kew, CO904/146).

4 *II*, 22 June 1921.

5 Ibid.

6 Ibid.

7 *Evening Herald*, 22 June 1921; *FJ*, 22 June 1921.

8 *II*, 22 June 1921.

9 Project Knockcroghery, *The burning of Knockcroghery, 1921*, contribution by Mary Murray-Dwyer at 57.35, available at www.youtube.com/watch?v= UnKf7NRJZgg, last accessed 25 Sept. 2021.

10 *RH*, 5 Nov. 1921.

11 Many of the descendants interviewed for the Project Knockcroghery documentary on the burning speak to the kindness of the rector and his wife and how this was spoken of in their families in the decades since the burning: see Project Knockcroghery, *The burning of Knockcroghery, 1921*, available at: www.youtube.com.

12 *RH*, 5. Nov. 1921.

13 *FJ*, 1 Nov. 1921.

14 *II*, 23 June 1921.

15 *RH*, 5 Nov. 1921.

16 *II*, 23 June 1921.

17 The presbytery had been built by Fr Bartley's brother, Fr Michael, during his tenure as parish priest of Knockcroghery between 1907 and 1919. For more, see *WI*, 2 Aug. 1919. See also Project Knockcroghery, *The burning*, Mary Murray-Dwyer's contribution at 30.46.

Some newspaper reports claim it was Fr Kelly's servants that extinguished the fire. It is not clear if Quigley was his housekeeper, but she did live across the road from the presbytery.

18 *II*, 23 June 1921.

19 Interview with Jimmy Murray by Declan Coyne, *Roscommon Champion 75th Anniversary Magazine* (Roscommon, 2003), pp 88–9.

20 Interview with Jimmy Murray, Coyne, p. 88. In his interview with Ernie O'Malley, Martin Fallon notes that 'June was an awfully dry month with several stations recording no rain for the month, an unusual occurrence in Ireland': Martin Fallon interview, UCD Archives, Ernie O'Malley Notebooks, p. 17b/131.

21 Interview with Jimmy Murray, Coyne, p. 88.

22 Ibid.

23 Project Knockcroghery, *The burning*, Mary Murray-Dwyer's contribution, 57.37.

24 Interview with Jimmy Murray, Coyne, p. 88.

25 Project Knockcroghery, *The burning*, Adrienne Colleran's contribution, 25.24.

26 Interview with Jimmy Murray, Coyne, p. 88.

27 *Daily Mirror*, 22 June 1921; *Birmingham Daily Gazette*, 22 June 1921; *Sheffield Daily Telegraph*, 22 June 1921. Each of these reports contained misinformation and stated that the village consisted of fifty houses.

28 *Indiana Daily Times*, 21 June 1921; *New York Times*, 22 June 1921; *Sydney Morning Herald*, 23 June 1921.

29 Joseph Devlin, 23 June 1921, *The parliamentary debates*, 5th ser., *House of Commons*, 1909–42 (cxliii, cc1531–3).

30 Project Knockcroghery, *The burning*, Michael Lyons' contribution, 42.19.

31 Interview with Jimmy Murray, Coyne, pp 88–9.

32 Extract from Benjamin Greene's diary, 18 Feb. 1922, transcribed by Mai Byrne, 'The diaries of Benjamin Greene of Hill House, Lecarrow – Part 2', *Rindoon Journal*, 2 (2005), pp 29–46 at p. 33.

33 Extract from Benjamin Greene's diary, 24 July 1922 and 26 Sept. 1922, Byrne, 'The diaries', pt 2, pp 40, 42.

4. THE AFTERMATH

1 *FJ*, 22 June 1921.
2 Ibid.
3 *Evening Echo*, 22 June 1921.
4 *FJ*, 22 June 1921.
5 *II*, 24 June 1921. See also Burke, *Athlone, 1900–23*, ch. 6.
6 *FJ*, 22 June 1921.
7 *II*, 24 June 1921. It is more likely that the remains were removed to St Mary's Church of Ireland church in Athlone, instead of St Peter's as reported by the *Irish Independent*.
8 *II*, 24 June 1921.
9 *II*, 22 June 1921; *FJ*, 22 June 1921.
10 *Pall Mall Gazette*, 6 Sept. 1921.
11 *FJ*, 17 Oct. 1921.
12 For more on the perspectives of the local press in the region, see Christopher Doughan, *The voice of the provinces: the regional press in revolutionary Ireland, 1914–1921* (Liverpool, 2019), pp 57–109.
13 *Yorkshire Post*, 22 June 1921.
14 War Office, *Record of the rebellion in Ireland*, iv, pp 54, 106.
15 King George V, speech to mark the opening of the Northern Irish parliament, Belfast, 22 June 1921, available at www.rte.ie/centuryireland/index.php/articles/the-kings-speech-in-belfast, last accessed 30 Nov. 2021.
16 *FJ*, 23 June 1921.
17 The four witnesses referred to here are Henry O'Brien, BMH, WS1308; Michael McCormack, BMH, WS1503; Thomas Costello, BMH, WS1296 and Frank O'Connor, BMH WS1309.
18 Thomas Costello, BMH, WS1296, p. 20.
19 Ibid.
20 Henry O'Brien, BMH, WS1308, p. 16.
21 *EE*, 21 June 1921.
22 *FJ*, 25 June 1921.
23 Thomas Costello, BMH, WS1296, p. 20. The local and national press also reported that some houses were burned at Mount Temple: see *WE*, 29 Oct. 1921 among others.
24 *WE*, 29 Oct. 1921.
25 Michael McCormack, BMH, WS1503, p. 32.
26 For more, see Terence Dooley, *Burning the big house: the story of the Irish country house in a time of war and rebellion* (New Haven, CT, 2022).
27 War Office, *Record of the rebellion in Ireland*, iv, p. 41.
28 Thomas Costello, BMH, WS1296, p. 20.
29 Dooley, *Burning the big house*, pp 110–13, 140–2.
30 Ibid. See also *WE*, 29 Oct. 1921 and *FJ*, 17 Oct. 1921.
31 Thomas Costello, BMH, WS1296, pp 20–1.
32 *WE*, 29 Oct. 1921.
33 Henry O'Brien, BMH, WS1308, p. 17.
34 *WE*, 29 Oct. 1921.
35 *WE*, 29 Oct. 1921; Thomas Costello, BMH, WS1296, p. 21.
36 *Offaly Independent*, 10 Mar. 1921.
37 *FJ*, 4 Aug. 1921.
38 Interview with Jimmy Murray, Coyne, p. 89.
39 Interview with Jimmy Murray by Riona Egan in *Rindoon Journal*, 1 (2004), pp 119–22 at p. 121.
40 Interview with Jimmy Murray, Coyne, p. 89.
41 *EE*, 2 Feb. 1921.
42 For more, see Adam Kidson, 'Quaker pacifism during the Irish Revolution', *Journal of the Friends Historical Society*, 1 (2007), pp 144–57 at p. 152; J. Anthony Gaughan (ed.), *Memoirs of Senator James G. Douglas: concerned citizen* (Dublin, 1998).
43 W.J. Williams, *Report of the Irish White Cross to 31 August 1922* (Dublin, 1922), p. 30.
44 Ibid., p. 28.
45 Ibid., p. 136.
46 Ibid., p. 138.
47 Ibid., p. 140.
48 *II*, 31 Oct. 1921.
49 *RH*, 5 Nov. 1921.
50 Ibid.
51 Ibid.; *II*, 29 Oct. 1921.
52 *II*, 31 Oct. 1921.
53 Information for this compensation record is sourced and compiled from the following: Roscommon Circuit Court, Criminal injuries book (National Archive of Ireland, Criminal injuries book, 1D/35/159); *II*, 29, 30 Oct. 1921; *WI*, 22 Jul. 1922; *Offaly Independent*, 10 Mar. 1923; *RH*, 21 Apr. 1923; *Iris Oifigiúil*, 3 Mar. 1923; *Iris Oifigiúil*, 18 Apr. 1923.

54 *RH*, 5 Nov. 1921.
55 Ibid.
56 David FitzPatrick, 'The price of Balbriggan' in David FitzPatrick (ed.), *Terror in Ireland, 1916–1923* (Dublin, 2012), pp 90–112 at p. 91.
57 *Offaly Independent*, 10 Mar. 1923.
58 *RJ*, 23 June 1921.

CONCLUSION
1 Thomas Costello, BMH, WS1296, p. 20.
2 This was referred to by Thomas Kelly in his BMH witness statement. Thomas Kelly, BMH, WS701, p. 9.
3 Hegarty-Thorne, *Flag a flyin'*, p. 105.
4 Ibid.
5 Patrick Lennon, BMH, WS1336, p. 13.